The Chilean Chronicles:

Moments and Memory
Forty Years After the Pinochet Coup

Jeff Kelly Lowenstein

ISBN: 978-0-9886817-3-6 (Print)
ISBN: 978-0-9886817-4-3 (Mobi)

Front Cover Photograph: Ana González, a human rights activist who had five relatives disappeared during the Pinochet dictatorship. *Photo courtesy Jon Lowenstein/NOOR, with support from the Pulitzer Center on Crisis Reporting.*
Back Cover Photograph: Jeff Kelly Lowenstein. *Photo courtesy of Grand Valley State University.*

Cover Design / Typesetting: Chris Moore www.fromprinttoebook.com

To the people of the paisito al sur del mundo.

I love you without knowing how, or when, or from where.
I love you straightforwardly, without complexities or pride;
so I love you because I know no other way

than this: where I does not exist, nor you,
so close that your hand on my chest is my hand,
so close that your eyes close as I fall asleep.

Pablo Neruda,
Sonnet XVII

"When you take this path of liberation… you know that
you can die at any moment. But those of us who remain
are not going to allow that to happen because forgetting
is death. Because of that, memory is essential."

Ana González,
Chilean human rights activist
who had five relatives disappeared
during the Pinochet dictatorship.

TABLE OF CONTENTS

An Introduction by Hugo Rojas

Searching for Memory and Social Justice in Chile:
Jeff Kelly Lowenstein in Action 8

Arrival

On the Plane and About to Land in Santiago, July 14, 2013 11

Settling in during July

Visiting La Chascona with Dunreith
and Margaret Woodman-Russell, July 19, 2013 14

Pure Magic with Alejandra, Alberto and Alejandro,
July 21, 2013 18

Donde Mi Negro, Lunchtime Courtesy of Cali, July 22, 2013 24

Joining the Kissing Couples, July 25, 2013 26

Señora Carmen and Chileans' View of the Nation's Past,
July 28, 2013 30

The Colors of Valparaíso, July 29, 2013 34

Juan in the Civil Registry, July 30, 2013 38

Building Community in August

Edmundo Verdugo Carnitas and the Treasures
of Quinta Vergara, August 1, 2013 40

Bar Liguria and the Power of Place, August 2, 2013 43

Maria Eliana and Humberto's Many Gifts, August 6, 2013 47

The End of Basque Week at the Estadio Español, August 7, 2013. . . 51

Meeting Dr. Juan Zuchel at Cerro San Cristóbal, August 17, 2013. . 55

Speaking about Dr. King and Dr. Bass at St. George's College,
August 19, 2013 61

A Grey Neruda Day Visiting Isla Negra, August 24, 2013 66

On Sylvia Broder's Courage, August 25, 2013 73

On Hugo Rojas' Longing for Pisco Sour and Ceviche,
August 29, 2013 76

Luis Dreams of a Home in Chillán, August 30, 2013 81

Charo Cofré's Many Skills, August 31, 2013 83

September 11

September 11 Countdown Begins, September 1, 2013 86

Memory at the Heart of a Divided Chile, September 2, 2013 89

The Week of Memory Begins, September 3, 2013 96

The Incomplete Victory of Villa Grimaldi, September 9, 2013 101

Memory Ceremony with Michelle Bachelet at Villa Grimaldi,
September 10, 2013 106

A Day of Memory in Three Parts, September 11, 2013 109

El Dieciocho

September 18 Celebrations Start in Providencia,
September 13, 2013 115

The Rodeo at Parque Alberto Hurtado, September 16, 2013 118

Meeting Patricio and Andrés at Estadio Nacional,
September 17, 2013 123

Terremoto 1, Jeff 0, September 18, 2013 129

Movies and Film

Patricio Guzmán's *Nostalgia for the Light*, August 18, 2013 133

Sebastián Lelio's *Gloria*, August 15, 2013 136

Los 80 Helps Chile Confront its Past, September 30, 2013 139

The 25th Anniversary of "No", October 8, 2013 142

Teaching

First Day Teaching Jitters, August 5, 2013 146

Zorba the Greek and My Data Journalism Class,
August 9, 2013 149

On My Own and My Students' Names, August 14, 2013 153

Students Progressing in Data Journalism Class, Channeling
Paul Tamburello, October 29, 2013 157

Data Journalism Class Ends, December 12, 2013 161

Memory

Meeting Juan Guzmán, October 20, 2013. 164

Hernán's Gutiérrez's Memory and Imagination,
December 4, 2013. 168

Mario Hernandez and Los Patitos, October 9, 2013 171

On Ángela Bachelet Jeria and Bearing Witness,
December 11, 2013 174

Working Toward a Better Chile

Viva La Mundial, October 16, 2013. 178

The Busy Life of Mayor Mario Gebauer, September 25, 2013 183

Carlo Gutiérrez and the Fight for Public Emails,
October 2, 2013 188

Rafael Gumucio's Book Launch, September 29, 2013 192

Striking Workers and Santiago's Central Markets,
August 16, 2013 196

Pamela Betancur's Unvanquished Dream, December 7, 2013 201

Return

Returning Home to Chicago, December 27, 2013. 205

Acknowledgments 210

About the Author 213

Searching for Memory and Social Justice in Chile: Jeff Kelly Lowenstein in Action

First impressions can be deceptive. An initial glance at this book may give the inaccurate impression that it is just a tale of the adventures of an American citizen who spent some months overseas. The truth is that this text is a lot more than that. Jeff Kelly Lowenstein's chronicles are an excellent account of current Chilean culture and society. Kelly Lowenstein not only gives a unique account on how Chileans commemorated the 40th anniversary of the military coup of 1973 and re-elected Michelle Bachelet as President of the Republic, he also recounts the stories of ordinary people with remarkable, often unnoticed, details. While conducting his research, he learned about the joys, pains, dreams and frustrations of many Chileans. The ideological polarization, urban segregation, classism and concentration of wealth, and the search for recognition by the victims of human rights violations, indigenous peoples and immigrants are topics that could not be absent in a text which purports to describe Chilean society. Kelly Lowenstein does not avoid these problems, yet he also illuminates the positive aspects of an institutionally and economically stable country.

Those of us who witnessed Kelly Lowenstein's work during his six-month stay in Chile were astounded by his curiosity, agility, objectivity and sense of story. Each time I spoke with Kelly Lowenstein, he invited me to offer my perceptions and to give explanations or reflect about the most diverse themes. Many of his conversation partners must have been amazed by his insatiable thirst for knowledge to learn about everything about Chile, from its great historical processes to the smallest details of its culture. That curiosity is not synonymous with naiveté, though. On the contrary, the characteristic skeptical attitude of a high-quality journalist was present in all of Kelly Lowenstein's dialogues.

Six months is a reasonable time to shape a general impression of a culture that you have recently come to know. However, it is also a period that can pass through your fingers if you don't keep track of the actions you plan and carry out. Kelly Lowenstein knew that he had to move quickly to get the greatest amount of information and impressions about the dilemmas and crossroads in Chilean society that he wanted to understand. Kelly Lowenstein discovered in his first month that it is not easy to understand the causes and consequences of the ideological divisions among Chileans. These chronicles show that he did not waste a day of his stay in the country. I always saw him ready to run tirelessly from one place to another, however many times were needed to reach his goal.

At the end of each day, while Kelly Lowenstein enjoyed his well-deserved rest, he also carved time to reflect and write in his blog about the day's events. The text you have in your hands is a revised edition of the posts he wrote every night and published on the Web. This reflective pause was the only permissible routine, because every day in Chile was an adventure that many would have liked to have. Perhaps he heard the voice of Gabriela Mistral:

"meditate in silence, enormous and dark, like a being who knows
of the pain of the world."

Kelly Lowenstein's generosity in sharing his notes with the readers invites us to leave our daily routine and perhaps exit our comfort zones, and to adopt the attitude of taking the risk of cultivating adventure in everyday life.

If these chronicles' immediacy betrays a sense of urgency, Kelly Lowenstein's ability to link the experiences and knowledge acquired in other moments in his life shows his analytical powers. The chronicles are objective and reflect what Kelly Lowenstein saw or heard. All of the information that appears in this book is true. As always, there are nuances and interpretations of observed facts, but everything Kelly Lowenstein has written corresponds with the reality that he lived. When walking by small streets, bars, classrooms and sites of memory, Kelly Lowenstein tried to show in his chronicles how protagonists are and how they think about their different stories. His extensive notes and photographs supplemented what he noticed and discussed. Indeed, a close reading of the chronicles reveals that each assertion he mentions is supported by multiple legitimate and verifiable sources.

Fresh and without literary pretensions, the chronicles are also an invitation to reflect on the meaning of our daily lives. Indeed, Kelly Lowenstein shows us that it is possible to assign special meaning to every one of our actions. The influence of his mentors, Paul Tamburello and Leon Bass, can be seen in the text. Ultimately these chronicles are an ode to life, the hope to transform everyday life into something extraordinary. Pablo Neruda synthesizes this attitude of searching in the *Canto General*: "Let me pursue my dream on your boundaries of sea and snow."

While these chronicles could have been written in any country, the most interesting aspect of the text is observing Kelly Lowenstein's capacity to prioritize and write about the most worthwhile activities. For example, I am sure that the teenage students to whom he spoke will never forget the talk he delivered about Dr. Martin Luther King, Jr. on the occasion of the fiftieth anniversary of King's iconic "I have a dream" speech. Rather they will recall the presentation with appreciation and respect. His students at Diego Portales University had the good fortune to improve their knowledge about transparency and access to public information. I trust that we will likely be surprised in the future by their audacious investigative work.

These chronicles would not have been possible without the support of Dunreith, his wife and life companion. The visits of his brother Jon, his son Aidan, his father Ed and Ed's partner, Lee Kass, also enabled Kelly Lowenstein to reflect collectively on the events he experienced. This text confirms that the embrace of family is essential to the proper development of any long-term project.

After seeing Kelly Lowenstein in action, I have to say that I came to a greater appreciation of the sensibility, agility, curiosity and objectivity of those journalists who legitimately seek to inform citizens in order to strengthen democracy and promote the culture of 'Never again'.

HUGO ROJAS
Professor of the Sociology of Law
Alberto Hurtado University

On the Plane and About to Land in Santiago

Posted on July 14, 2013

We're almost there.

Thirteen years after I first applied to the Fulbright program, six months after we began the process of preparing to sell our home, and one day after countless trips in and out of the house, we are an hour or so from landing in Santiago, Chile.

Dunreith, my wife, who is sitting next to me on an unusually cold plane ride, and I will be spending more than five months there.

I've been selected to be a Fulbright Scholar at Diego Portales University. While there, I'll teach a class on data journalism, offer a lecture series to other members of the department about the work we do with data, conduct research about the impact of a landmark 2009 freedom of information law, and work to serve as a bridge between my Chilean colleagues and people I know who do the same work in Spanish- and non-Spanish speaking countries.

I'll also be doing some freelance work for *Hoy*, the *Chicago Tribune's* Spanish-language newspaper where I've worked since March 2011. I'll chronicle where things stand in the country that is just a generation removed from a brutal dictatorship, learn how better to write computer code, and work on some personal projects.

And, when it's over, I get my fulltime job back at *Hoy*.

To be able to go to another land is an enormous gift; to be able to do so with job security is even greater. Returning to *Hoy* and working at a place that supports this kind of striving and professional growth are just two of the many reasons I'm thrilled about the experience.

In fact, we've wanted to go to the land of Nobel literature laureates Pablo Neruda and Gabriela Mistral for more than a decade.

Dear friend, poet, human rights activist and generous soul Marjorie Agosín, a Chilean native who was a teenager in Athens, Georgia when the coup that toppled the democratically-elected Salvador Allende from power took place, has been our inspiration and our guide about her homeland.

Dunreith and I read Neruda's Sonnet XVII to each other during our elopement and our subsequent public marriage ceremony at Look Park:

I do not love you as if you were salt-rose, or topaz, or the arrow of carnations the fire shoots off. I love you as certain dark things are to be loved, in secret, between the shadow and the soul.

I love you as the plant that never blooms but carries in itself the light of hidden flowers; thanks to your love a certain solid fragrance, risen from the earth, lives darkly in my body.

I love you without knowing how, or when, or from where. I love you straightforwardly, without complexities or pride; so I love you because I know no other way

than this: where I does not exist, nor you, so close that your hand on my chest is my hand, so close that your eyes close as I fall asleep.

There is the chance to explore the nation's trauma from the Pinochet era that Chilean documentary film director Patricio Guzmán depicted so hauntingly in his film, *Nostalgia for the Light*.

As someone who counts attending South Africa's Truth and Reconciliation Commission (TRC) in 1996 as a major life moment, I've studied the Chilean version of the TRC that was held earlier than the one in South Africa, but didn't go nearly as long or probe as deeply. Now I will have more of a chance.

There is the opportunity for Dunreith and me to truly immerse ourselves in Spanish.

Dunreith and I are also excited to have this adventure as the first chapter in a new stage of our lives.

After months of decluttering and painting and fixing and staging and showing and inspecting and appraising, we sold our house yesterday.

This means that we've got no home address in the United States. It also means that we're free in a way that we've not been for the past decade.

We've loved the house in many ways. It's where we've spent the vast majority of our married life, the place where we raised our son Aidan from a boy to a man, where we both turned 45 and Dunreith turned 50.

We lived at 1509 South Boulevard while Dunreith's parents Marty and Helen and my stepmother Diane faltered before passing. It's the location where Aidan has lived longer than anywhere else. And yet, for years really, and especially after Aidan graduated from high school and attended Tulane, the house has felt larger and more expansive than what we needed.

As of Wednesday morning, it belongs to someone else.

Selling the house and setting off to Chile is not just the beginning of a new chapter. It's more confirmation that we can indeed live a life of choosing each day what we want to do and how we want to do it, that we can align our deepest dreams and most basic values with our daily actions, and that, while the end will inevitably come, it is possible to savor richly layered moments of joy in which we appreciate the past, work to the future and always, always live in the present.

I can look across Dunreith and out the window and see the snow-capped Andes in the distance.

We land in 10 minutes.

Our adventure has already begun.

Visiting La Chascona with Dunreith and Margaret Woodman-Russell

Posted on July 19, 2013

Alejandra Fritz was our guide at La Chascona.
(Photo courtesy of Jeff Kelly Lowenstein)

If there was ever any shred of a doubt that Pablo Neruda, nee Neftalí Ricardo Reyes, lived an epic, fantastical life, it can be permanently eradicated by visiting La Chascona in Santiago's Bellavista neighborhood.

That's the name that the legendary Chilean poet, diplomat, communist and global citizen gave to his third and final house. (The other two are in nearby Valparaíso and Isla Negra.) The title was bestowed in honor of

Matilde Urrutia, his lover at the time construction on the house began in 1953. It refers to the nickname he gave the actress, who eventually became his third wife after Neruda and Delia del Carril divorced, due to her abundant, unruly and overflowing red hair.

The house eventually had three distinct buildings that were completed over the course of five years.

Each bore the influence of Neruda, who worked with Catalan architect Germán Rodríguez Arias on the first two sections, and with Chilean architect Carlos Martner on the final section.

Alejandra Fritz, a former literature student who now works in publishing, guided my wife Dunreith, Margaret Woodman-Russell, daughter of dear friend Dave Russell, and a handful of others on the English language tour.

Alejandra explained that Neruda wanted each area of the house to feel like a boat—a desire that was based in large part on his complicated relationship with water. (He learned to swim only when he was 50 years old, she said, so he wanted to feel like he was in water but on land.)

Objective accomplished.

The first room had the narrow shape of a boat, wooden floors that creaked ominously at times, and a spiral staircase that took us up to the second floor and a second section of the house designed to resemble a lighthouse.

It, along with all the other spaces we visited, had artifacts from Neruda's decades as a diplomat and examples of his willingness to indulge his habit of being a "thinger", not a collector.

We are talking dolls from Poland. The first robots in world history from 17th century France that were clad in Turkish outfits. A miniature horse from India. A pair of giant shoes from an area shoe store.

A pair of weight reduction belts that Don Pablo used in his ongoing battles against the bulge. (Even a casual student of the master knows how much he loved food from his odes to salt, fried potatoes and the onion.)

Rows of eyes hanging down from the ceiling and in the garden encouraged you to take in whatever was around you.

At the same time, while the house bears Neruda's imprint, it shows Matilde's influence, too.

She not only lived there for a dozen years after Neruda's death—he died just 12 days after the coup that drove Socialist President Salvador Allende to suicide and initiated the destructive reign of Gen. Augusto Pinochet—

but also worked tirelessly on the trees and plants that envelop the home in cool, clear air.

Portraits of the former actress appear throughout the house.

In the bedroom they shared, a formal portrait shows her with the hair that earned the house its name and wearing an elegant, off-the-shoulder dress.

In another part of the house Mexican muralist and longtime Neruda friend Diego Rivera painted a portrait of Matilde with two heads, a reference, Alejandra explained, to the public role of friend that she played while Neruda was still married to his Argentine second wife. Matilde's middle name was Rosario, and Rivera said that one face represented Matilde, while the other part embodied Rosario. The muralist noted the relationship's originally clandestine nature by drawing the poet's face and profile in one part of Matilde's bushy hair.

Other pictures of Neruda are far less subtle.

El Poeta depicts the celebration that Allende held in the national soccer stadium after Neruda won the 1971 Nobel Prize for Literature. In the image, Neruda sits in profile in front of the tens of thousands of ant-like people who have come to celebrate his honor. His eyes contain the Andes mountains.

There's also a photograph of Neruda from the time he was in Capri, a period when his politics led him to be exiled from his homeland and a place like the one in Antonio Skármeta's novel where a fictional Neruda met a humble postman seeking for language to express his love for the woman he later married. The poet's encouragement of the young man in his quest became the subject of the Academy Award-winning film, *Il Postino*.

Beyond the things Neruda collected and the artwork that hangs on the wall, La Chascona is also a place of people, and his life intersected with many of the last century's brightest stars.

In the field of art, in addition to his connection with Rivera, he was friends with Magritte and Picasso.

In politics, Willy Brandt was a Nobel Prize winner for Peace in the same year that Neruda claimed the Literature Prize.

For literature, he dined with Hemingway and received English lessons from Arthur Miller to help him deliver a lecture at Oxford University.

This all in a place where Alejandra explained that he did not even spend the majority of his time.

La Chascona was ransacked in the days after the coup that occurred on Sept. 11, 1973, and close to a third of its materials were destroyed. The end of the Allende regime devastated Neruda, who was suffering from prostate cancer.

But he was not so weak that he was unable to inform armed forces who were searching the home at Isla Negra where he spent the greatest amount of time: "Look around—there's only one thing of danger for you here—poetry."

Images of Neruda's funeral fill one part of a room in the third section of the house.

Mourners led by Matilde started near the home. With the crowd of thousands who joined, they marched to the Recoleta neighborhood where the great poet was laid to rest.

The march was the first protest against the new regime, Alejandra told us. After her husband's death and a brief period of departure from the country, Matilde worked on behalf of the thousands of people who were disappeared during the Pinochet regime

In the end, Pinochet was forced from power, while Neruda's poetry and the near magical appeal of his homes endure.

We can't wait to see the other two.

Pure Magic with
Alejandra, Alberto and Alejandro

Posted on July 21, 2013

Toasting with new friends.
(Photo courtesy of Jeff Kelly Lowenstein)

If you're lucky in your life, you'll have the chance to experience days that feel like pure magic, as if an enchanted air has descended from the sky and cast a glorious spell over you and everyone around you.

Saturday was one of those days for Dunreith and me. We spent the afternoon and a large part of the evening in the company and at the home of Alejandra Matus, Alberto Barrera and their five-year-old son Alejandro. Alejandra and Alberto are highly unusual people.

She is a fierce and decorated journalist who, in a country whose press has often been criticized as being excessively acquiescent and docile to oppressive authority, has written important books about the 1976 assassination of Chilean ambassador Orlando Letelier by the Pinochet government and about the nepotism, corruption and lack of independence that existed within the judiciary during the Pinochet era.

All copies of the latter work were ordered confiscated the day after it was published in 1999, a full nine years after Pinochet had left power.

Beyond that, the government sought to prosecute Alejandra under a Chilean law that forbade citizens and journalists from offending officials. If convicted, Alejandra faced five years in prison. She asked for, and received, asylum, from the United States. She stayed in our country for more than two years, returning only after the law under which she would have been prosecuted had been overturned.

Last year, after an additional two years in the United States—a time during which she was a Nieman Fellow and earned a Master's degree in Public Administration from the Harvard Kennedy School of Government—she joined the faculty at Diego Portales University where I will be teaching.

During her Nieman year Alejandra was a classmate with Beth Macy, an intrepid and award-winning reporter, author of the forthcoming book *Factory Man*, and a friend from the Ochberg Society for Trauma Journalism. Beth gave me Alejandra's contact information shortly before I left and suggested I reach out to her upon my arrival.

Alberto, who hails from the town of Antofagasta in the northern part of Chile, is a veteran Socialist activist who left the country at age 17 during the Pinochet dictatorship. He went first to Bolivia, then spent six months in Brazil and three years in Norway. Later he lived for three years in Frankfurt, Germany. During these years he continued his organizing work against the brutal regime, occasionally being smuggled in and out of his homeland whose security forces would have killed him had they caught him.

The oldest of nine children, Alberto often received help from one of his brothers, a hairdresser in Argentina who would cut Alberto's hair in a way that would disguise his identity.

Dunreith and I met Alejandra in person on Thursday, and she invited us to her home on Saturday. This morning, we set off close to noon.

After a Metro ride to the Central Station, we found and then took a bus down a largely straight road through increasingly rural territory before the bus driver informed us we had arrived at Paradero 36.5 in the community of Lonquén.

Alejandra and her son Alejandro, who has straight black hair, bunches of curiosity, a few missing teeth and a voice that is accustomed to being heard, picked us up and drove us up a twisty and bumpy dirt road to their home that is nestled in the Andes mountains.

We walked up a winding set of wooden slats with raised steps to guide us and arrived at the farmhouse-style home Alejandra designed after purchasing a large plot of land a decade ago. Although I've recently extolled the virtues of living in a small space, I have to admit that entering a home with high triangular ceilings was a pleasure. So, too, was walking past a handmade vintage wooden table and settling near a fire that was well stoked, if not blazing, in front of three couches that, along with the fireplace, formed a square. While putting the finishing touches on squash filled with local cheese, Alejandra offered us our first pisco sour, a tart lemony concoction.

Alberto and I chatted about his time in exile. He said that he lost many friends during the dictatorship. The terror was not rational, he explained. Friends and family who were not political were tortured and killed, while others who were openly against the regime survived. His father was among that number. Alberto's dad was a staunch opponent of the regime who was absent from the northern community of Antofagasta when the coup occurred.

Alberto said his father was away for the first few months of the regime, and thus escaped being killed in the Caravan of Death, one of the first waves of murdering political opponents. Although he was stripped of his teaching position and thus had to scramble to do all kinds of jobs during the dictatorship, his father never left the country. The school gave him his job back when Pinochet's reign ended. Alberto had not seen his father for 11 years when Pinochet left power in 1990. It would be another three before he saw him again. By that time, when Alberto returned, many of his former comrades had become part of the governmental leadership.

Alberto called Jorge, an employee who has his own house on the property and works a few hours a day, to help him light the fire on the grill that he cleaned with half of a fresh onion.

Those tasks completed, he put out a thick slab of virtually fat free beef, and added liberal doses of salt.

Alejandro watches his father on the grill.
(Photo courtesy of Jeff Kelly Lowenstein)

Alejandra and Dunreith brought out the squash, creamed garbanzo beans, brown rice and a tangy beet salad the two of them prepared and that had left purple stains on their hands.

The air was far cleaner and fresher than in Santiago, where a higher number of people than usual were wearing masks to ward off the air pollution.

Alberto continued to pour, and we continued to drink goblets full of rich red Chilean wine. He told us we were in training for the September celebrations of Chilean independence, which last a week and involve large portions of Diego Portales University journalism faculty gathering, drinking copious amounts of wine and dancing.

I told Alejandra that we had planned to go to Argentina during the break, but that perhaps we would change our plans. "You should," she said, laughing. We munched contentedly on the feast in front of us until we had had enough, then ate some more. After a while we decided to follow Alejandro, who had gone inside because he was too cold to stay at the table.

"Do you eat like this every day?" I asked Alejandra on the way into the house.

"Not every day," she answered. "But most weekends we do something, because otherwise it would be a waste."

We each took a place on the couch and settled in for what turned out to be hours and hours of wide ranging conversation in Spanish and English over a luscious cheese-cake like dessert, tea or coffee—I had the former, while everyone else had the latter—and, of course, as many more glasses of wine as we were willing to consume.

The topics flowed from Alejandra's years of exile following the publication of *The Black Book of Chilean Justice* to the comparative ineffectiveness of the Transparency Law passed in 2009 during President Michelle Bachelet's tenure to the shared military background of Bachelet and Evelyn Matthei, both daughters of Air Force generals and childhood friends who now are presidential opponents.

We spoke about the concentration of wealth that became even greater during the dictatorship to the materialism that has crept into Chilean society and *Paula*, a feminist magazine that's been around nearly half a century and to which Alejandra contributed a recent story about her mother. She told us about her upcoming book, while Alberto shared about their travels around the United States.

Together we discussed the similarities and differences between Chile and South Africa, countries that are still emerging from the wounds they sustained during the period of authoritarian government that ended in the early 90s. In short, it was a virtual primer and seminar on Chilean history, the dictatorship and life afterward from two people who had lived through and fought against it in distinct, yet related ways.

Eventually, Alejandro started to hit what Dunreith used to call "Mambo Time," that point in the day that parents the world over confront where the window to have a smooth bedtime has closed because of adults enjoying being with each other.

Alejandro kissed us goodbye. We hugged Alberto and shared intentions of getting together again soon. Alejandra drove us to the bus stop for our return journey and waited with her blinkers flashing until we got on the right one. We didn't wave vigorously enough to flag down the first bus that roared by the stop that was covered in darkness, but did so the second time.

Dunreith and I both dozed off in the bus even though the lights were on. A young Chilean signaled for us to join everyone else and leave when we arrived at the last stop. It had been a day not so much when hope and history rhyme, as Seamus Heaney would say, but rather where food and drink and mutual values and relationships and a spirit of openness and acceptance combined to create an exquisite moment of shared connection.

My ever deeper understanding of life's permanently fleeting nature, the 13 years since I first applied to the Fulbright program, the dozen years since Dunreith and I first identified that we wanted to go to Chile, and the memories of the generosity my friends in South Africa showed me 18 years ago all made my appreciation and gratitude that much more profound.

So, too, did the awareness of being firmly in the middle of life, and of the enormous gift of meeting kindred spirits in different, yet similar places on their journeys. At this point we all have aging or deceased parents, children at varying stages of being grown, careers and passions having been chosen, and former lovers and spouses. Because of all this, we are acutely aware of the preciousness of any moment, let alone such a rich one as this.

We walked back through the bus station, back onto the crowded Metro that, as it always does, zipped us back to the Pedro de Valdivia stop that is rapidly becoming homelike for us.

It was raining harder than it has since we arrived, but the magic of the day shielded us and made us feel like we were dodging the drops.

Donde Mi Negro, Lunchtime Courtesy of Cali

Posted on July 22, 2013

Two years ago Judith Torres couldn't find work in her native Cali, Colombia, so she decided to search better fortune for herself and her two sons in Santiago.

Shortly after her arrival Torres decided to open Donde Mi Negro, a restaurant serving typical Colombian fare on the corner of Herrera and Agustinas streets, right near major thoroughfare Matakuna Street.

Torres' pride in her roots can be seen in the image of a curvy woman in a yellow bikini who stands in a heart of the national colors of yellow, red and blue above the wooden doors and graffiti-stained orange walls through which you enter to find a clean and modest space that seats about two dozen people. Dunreith and I ate at the restaurant for lunch today after we had entered the Museum of Memory and Human Rights and decided we needed to take the sights and sounds in on a full stomach.

We had already met with Diego Portales University department chair Carlos Aldunate and other colleagues like project coordinator Josefa Romero and academic secretary Loreto Correa. Josefa told us that the school has the largest journalism department in the country; judging from the resources there, the school is well equipped to train the next generation of aspiring broadcast, radio and print/digital scribblers.

The Colombian flag also appears in the middle of the menu, which more than delivers the standard, reasonably-priced dishes promised at the restaurant's entrance. Dunreith had a cheese empanada that was more heavily fried than the Chilean varieties we've sampled thus far for a mere 50 cents, while I had a full quarter chicken for $2.40 accompanied by a hefty plate of piping hot and glistening French Fries for an additional 80 cents.

A salad with large tomato slices, generous portions of cauliflower and some broccoli atop lettuce was an unexpected surprise.

Torres, who learned to cook from her mother and at a cooking institute in Cali, was plying her trade on a four-burner stove with a hefty black frying pan going to work on beautifully-rounded papa rellenas, a skillet with lean pork chops and a hefty pot waiting on the side in reserve.

The crowd of primarily working class people—there was a heavy presence of men wearing blue jeans and paint-splattered sweatshirts and sneakers with holes—ate in contented silence. Judith said that her customers are not only Colombian, but come from many different countries.

She does not work alone. Aurora Huauaco pitches in with cooking and waiting on tables, and Sandra Paola Torres serves the customers, too.

Judith convinced her younger of two sisters and the baby of five children who also could not find work in Cali to join her in Santiago five months ago.

"I paved the way and then she joined me," Judith said with a laugh.

The sisters work together on weekdays from 10:00 a.m. to 7:00 p.m., and Judith keeps the place open on weekends, too.

Two years after she arrived, although she has good days and bad days, Judith is optimistic that things are heading in the right direction. She plans to stay in Santiago with her boys, who are 15 and four years old.

Not Sandra. "I want to go to the United States," she told me in Spanish. "Put me in your suitcase, but take me. With urgency."

Joining the Kissing Couples

Posted on July 25, 2013

Couples like this inspired me on Wednesday.
(Photo courtesy of Jeff Kelly Lowenstein)

We had already walked for an hour and a half on a dusty and unseasonably hot winter day here in Santiago, so Dunreith's primary goal in finding a green bench and sitting down for a few minutes in Parque Balmaceda was to have a quick rest before finishing the trek back to our apartment.

I, however, had another objective: to join the kissing couples.

They are everywhere in Santiago's public spaces. Some lie in the grass near the Mapocho River. Others stretch across each other in Parque Uruguay. Still others intertwine their limbs in every conceivable way on the benches that are identical in design to the one on which we had just sat.

But whatever their differences may be in position and location, they share a fundamental similarity: they embrace each other with abandon.

Tender head-holding and hair-stroking. Soulful glances offered and received whenever the eyes are open. Quiet words issued inches from the partner's lips.

At the same time, these couples exhibit a restraint that has within it a certain elegance. Clothes stay on at all times, and the awareness that they are indeed in a public setting can be seen by an occasional blush or raised eyebrow when one walks past them.

The vast majority of the couples appear to be on the young side.

I'm not an expert in discerning age, but my best guess is that many, if not most, are in the teenage to twentysomething range. While almost all of them are straight, we have noticed a few lesbian and gay sets of partners, too.

I've not yet spoken to any of the couples locked in embrace, so I don't have much insight as to whether they are doing so because they don't have anywhere else to go—many Chileans live at home until their 30s, I have read—or because they are simply expressing their inner emotions.

I just knew that I wanted to be one of them for a minute or two.

I turned to Dunreith, put my arm around her shoulder, swiveled suavely, placed my face inches from hers and declared, "Entiendo tu plan."

I understand your plan. (As part of my commitment to Spanish immersion, I often speak the language to Dunreith these days in our apartment and on the streets.)

"You're a caricature," she told me, even as her eyebrows arched and her eyes held just a hint of a smile.

I couldn't imagine what she was talking about.

"How could you say this?" I asked in Spanish.

My question sparked a discussion for several minutes in which Dunreith asserted that I speak in exaggerated tones and gesture when I talk in Spanish with her, especially when I am seeking romance.

To be fair, I did do the bulk of my initial learning how to speak Spanish from the Mexican telenovela *Destilando Amor*, a story of a farm worker and a tequila scion who fall in love with each other.

Thus, in the early stages of my use of the language, I was prone to issuing hyperbolic statements to Dunreith like, "Ti quiero con un amor tan limpio y puro como el mundo nunca ha visto."

I love with you a love so pure and clean like the world has never seen.

I learned in ensuing interactions with actual Spanish speakers that, while they liked the story of how I had learned to speak their native tongue, it was in fact not necessary to use either such language or a tone that could accurately be characterized as well over the top.

I thought I had kicked that proverbial habit, but was hearing from my wife that indeed this was not the case. Of course, her desire to rest may have affected how she heard and interpreted my request.

Dunreith and I first met 16 years ago this month at a Facing History follow up seminar at the organization's Brookline headquarters. We got together a year later and have been with each other ever since.

One of the qualities that most attracted me to Dunreith from the beginning of our relationship was our ability to talk. We would do so for hours each evening on the phone—at the time, she was living in Western Massachusetts, while I was in Brighton- and even more during the weekends, when I would drive out to spend time with Aidan and her.

The other was her generosity. Time and time again, particularly in moments of pain and disappointment, she would reach within herself and find a way to make a gesture that showed that she understood and valued me.

I moved in close and told Dunreith again in Spanish how I felt about her.

This time, instead of resisting, she smiled.

In that instant I saw the same smile she had given when I requested that she sit down on the grey striped Ottoman she'd owned for 20 years and asked her to spend her life with me.

Then she closed her eyes and moved her lips toward me.

We kissed.

The kiss was not of the same length or intensity as the Chilean couples we had seen, walked past or nearly stepped on—I'm not kidding when I say that they are everywhere—but it moved me into the club nevertheless.

A little later, we kissed again.

After that we sat on the bench for a while.

Although still high in the sky, the sun had begun its descent. The sounds of cars whizzing by on the afternoon commute on Andrés Bello behind us were reinforced by an occasional horn and the whir of cars in front of us on Providencia Avenue.

A couple with a newborn baby chatted quietly as they walked by us, the father with the baby snugly against his chest while the mother carried a blue cloth bag with the word "Baby" stitched on the side in white letters. So did a pair of adolescent girls still dressed in their school uniform of a pleated skirt and dark tights. Bicycles with large tires crunched over the gravel.

A happiness filled me in a way that it rarely had before.

It was a joy that came from being fully in that moment of all five senses with my beloved, the woman with whom I have made a life and raised a son and nursed and buried parents and seen physical changes and known disappointment and traveled the earth and realized dreams.

We didn't kiss as long as many of the Chilean couples.

But we were among them.

And it was perfect.

Señora Carmen and Chileans' View of the Nation's Past

Posted on July 28, 2013

Señora Carmen at Santiago's Biblioplaza.
(Photo courtesy of Jeff Kelly Lowenstein)

If there was one idea I had firmly committed in my mind before arriving in Chile, it was this: the people in the country agreed that the Pinochet dictatorship was bad.

Based on wrenching accounts of disappeared, tortured and murdered people, buttressed by a diet of books, poems, films and new programs, I had a picture of an unspeakably repressive military regime that controlled its people by sheer force. The United States government saw in Gen.

Augusto Pinochet, as it did with the Somoza family in Nicaragua and Shah Reza Pahlavi in Iran, an anticommunist bulwark and ally, however unsavory.

A couple of weeks into my stay here, the picture is becoming more complex.

The loosening of my viewpoint first came through watching *The Judge and the General*, Elizabeth Farnsworth and Patricio Lanfranco's award-winning documentary film. The movie depicts how Judge Juan Guzmán, left the insular right-wing world in which he had allowed himself to live, and immersed himself in the gruesome details of the Pinochet regime. Guzmán ultimately indicted the man who had been largely responsible for his professional ascent.

The film opens and closes with footage of Pinochet's coffin being carried onto the street after the dictator died without having been prosecuted or convicted of the crimes that impacted so many Chilean families.

Then-President Michelle Bachelet, herself a torture survivor, exile and the the nation's first female president, refused to declare Pinochet's death a national day of mourning.

Her decision prompted an outpouring of venomous yelling and epithet throwing from hundreds, if not thousands, of Pinochet supporters who cursed their newly-elected leader and chanted, "They never got him!" A dismayed Guzmán speaks while watching footage of the protests about the division that clearly existed within the country: "It's still there."

That is the conclusion I drew after talking Tuesday with Señora Carmen, an energetic and friendly retired elementary school teacher who taught for 17 years in one of Santiago's most impoverished neighborhoods. Dunreith and I met her Wednesday on the way to registering our visas within the required 30-day period.

Dressed smartly in a black jacket and orange scarf, Señora Carmen was manning the city's Biblioplaza right near the National Fine Arts Museum. Established about 10 years ago, the facility has books and newspapers available for residents to take out and return.

Carmen, who is energetic and friendly, explained that she would teach the same students for four consecutive years from first to fourth grades. That continuity was important, she said, because many of the students grew up in a drug-filled environment in a poor neighborhood in Santiago.

"You must have been like a mother to many of those students," I said.

She agreed.

I told her about Dunreith having been an educator for many years as well as about my late mother-in-law Helen, who taught and was an elementary school principal during her 34 years in education.

I also told her about my experience of working as an apprentice for two years in former fourth grade teacher Paul Tamburello's class, the same classroom where I had been a student a dozen years earlier. "He felt that was the ultimate example of impact," I said, adding that last year I published a book called *On My Teacher's Shoulders* about learning from Paul at three different points in my life.

"Que buena," Señora Carmen answered, a smile filling her face as her eyes danced with delight.

"I imagine that you hear from former students," I said.

She said that she did.

"How are they doing?" I asked.

"Some are doing well; others are not doing well," she replied, a shadow of sadness crossing her face.

"It's gotten worse in the past 10 years," she said.

"Worse?" I asked.

She repeated her answer.

"It was better during the dictatorship. Things were more controlled," she added. "There was respect."

I explained that we had always heard in the United States that things were worse during the Pinochet era.

Señora Carmen's face started to harden in resistance.

"But you are telling me that you think it was better then," I said.

"It was better," she said again with conviction.

"You have taught me something," I said. "Thank you."

We started to leave, but Señora Carmen asked me to write down my name.

Dunreith asked if I had a business card. I started to open my backpack and look for one. But Señora Carmen said she only wanted my name to remember the conversation, which she had enjoyed. I took one of the book receipts and wrote my name in capital letters as neatly as I could.

I told her that, as opposed to Chile, where people carry both their mother and father's name, but go by their paternal lineage, our last name was Kelly Lowenstein.

I had been Lowenstein.

She had been Kelly.

Together we were Kelly Lowenstein.

We also have two names, Señora Carmen said.

We thanked her again, shook hands and took one more picture before heading on our way to the police department where we were required to register our visas, my understanding of Chilean people's attitude toward their country's past slightly muddier than before Señora Carmen and I began to talk.

The Colors of Valparaíso

Posted on July 29, 2013

One of many murals throughout Valparaíso.
(Photo courtesy of Jeff Kelly Lowenstein)

Valparaíso explodes in brilliant, luminous, pastel colors everywhere you turn.

The buildings.

The worker's clothes.

The street art.

The garage doors.

The skyline as the sun falls in the late afternoon.

The murals and graffiti that seem to spring up, like roots through concrete, throughout the seaport city that has been a harbor for centuries.

Even the dogs.

The city that seems like a cross between the hilly, twisting streets of San Francisco and ocean views of Haifa, Israel, was the first place we visited outside of the Santiago area.

It's got a gritty side, to be sure.

Scores of abandoned canines leave their droppings everywhere in the city. We saw two of them feasting on rotted meat they had ripped open from garbage bags.

And when Dunreith and I asked a pair of adolescent girls about where to get an empanada, they told us that an area where we had planned to go was "Super peligro."

Super dangerous.

But, still, those colors.

We arrived in the city around noon. After an engaging conversation with yet another of our friend Marjorie Agosín's seemingly unending stream of cousins, it was approaching two o'clock and we hadn't eaten lunch. We walked up a street that, like many in Valparaíso, wound around, rather than going in a straight line, to Almacen Nacional, a restaurant recommended by the ibis hotel at which we were staying and a place where we received a 10 percent discount.

More colors.

From the bright blue painting on the wall of a couple in bed, to the bar, which was a symphony in muted tones, to the green zucchini soup topped with a slice of the vegetable, to the flaming red hair of the woman at the table next to us, to the pink lipstick our waitress wore.

We had a meal with service that could charitably be called relaxed, then ambled around Avenida Alemania, or Germany, taking in panoramic views of the harbor until we arrived at La Sebastiana, the second of fabled poet Pablo Neruda's homes we've seen since arriving here 15 days ago.

The information in the audio guide was sparse compared with the rich descriptions we had received from Alejandra Fritz at La Chascona, Neruda's home in Santiago's Bella Vista neighborhood. Nevertheless, the house inspired a similar, if deeper yet slightly emotionally subdued, understanding not just of Neruda's fantastic life, but his incessant capacity for creativity.

The sun started its inexorable descent.

Dunreith suggested that we go back in a more direct way that took us down uneven stairs, through little traveled pathways. We walked past a mother kneeling to tie her son's sneakers and dusty workers standing wearily on the front steps of their homes.

A trio of young men whose picture I had taken on the way down thanked me. One thrust an open beer toward me and asked me if I wanted it. "I'm with my woman," I said pointing to Dunreith, who had walked ahead, as she often does when I am using the camera. "But if not, then yes."

We laughed.

"Coca Cola?" another asked as I moved past them.

We all laughed again.

A street lamp and telephone wire framed the streaks of pink that poked over the top of the buildings before the sun disappeared for the evening. We continued walking through a dicey area, drawn through it by the insistent thumping of bass drums. A crowd had gathered in a town square to hear a local youth band perform. Five girls shimmied provocatively in the front row.

The band leader with his arms aloft.
(Photo courtesy of Jeff Kelly Lowenstein)

The yellow-shirted leader in the middle of the group raised his arms as if in victory. Everyone in the band shouted, "Val-pa-ra-í-so!" The crowd burst into applause and started to disperse into the darkness of the night that enveloped the city like a glove.

Dunreith found a supermarket where we bought fruit and red wine to keep alive our streak of drinking every night in Chile. She stopped on the street near the hotel to buy a colorful assortment of mints and jellied candies.

Drink, dessert and rest, if not dinner, awaited, just hundreds of yards away.

Juan in the Civil Registry

Posted on July 30, 2013

We were about halfway through the line at the civil registry when Juan sat on the blue plastic seat next to me and calmly used his small spoon to dish out his vanilla and chocolate-flavored dessert in an unhurried manner.

A din of cell phones ringing, babies crying, and names being called surrounded us.

A sea of people from Africa, Asia, Peru, Colombia, Mexico, the United States and Spain, among others, waited, all of us silently willing the bureaucrats behind the desks to go faster so that our turn would come. (We were there to have our visas certified.)

"How old are you?" I asked him.

"Nine," answered Juan, who was short, had thick black hair and wore a dark blue sweatsuit.

"You look like you're 10," I told him, using my standard line with children. He shook his head." No, I'm nine."

"What are you eating?"

"A little sweet," he said. "Do you want some?"

"No, thank you," I said, touched. "When did you move here?"

The question required Juan to consult with his mother, a smiling woman with shoulder-length brown hair and wearing blue jeans.

"Four months," he told me after he secured the information.

"How do you like it?"

"A little," he said.

"When our son was nine years old, we moved from a state called Massachusetts to a place called Chicago in Illinois that he liked a little after four months, I said. "Have you heard of it?"

"I saw it in a film," he answered.

"I don't know if this will be your experience, but he decided years later that he liked it better where we had moved to than where we used to live," I told him.

I started to elaborate on this idea, but Juan's mother beckoned him to come over to her. He trotted off obediently, and I turned my attention back to writing.

A few minutes Juan stood in front of me.

He extended his hand, a smile crossing his face.

I shook it and wished him luck.

"I believe in you," I called after Juan's retreating form.

I don't know if he heard me.

He rejoined his mother and followed her as they waded through the sea of humanity in the impossibly crowded room. They walked out of the door and into the rest of their lives.

The memory of Aidan at nine when we moved from the only place he had ever lived trailed behind them.

Edmundo Verdugo Carnitas and the Treasures of Quinta Vergara

Posted on August 1, 2013

Edmundo Verdugo Carnitas before he started dancing.
(Photo courtesy of Jeff Kelly Lowenstein)

Quinta Vergara park in Viña del Mar has many treasures.

There are the large stone plaques that greet you when you pass through the black gates and that honor Gabriela Mistral and Pablo Neruda, Chile's pair of Nobel laureates for literature.

There are the paths that wind up and down the park.

Filled with leafy green spaces that spark memories of the California redwoods, they provide shelter from the sun, a cocoon of cool, clear air and the perfect environment for a lengthy, leisurely stroll to consider and start to discuss one of life's most fundamental questions: what do we want to do and to have done with our time on the planet?

There are the stones placed artfully around the garden, each with poems or poem fragments by bards through Central and South America that invite you to engage with their words, their images and the images about the single conversation that matters most—life.

There are the leaves sculpted with skill and precision into the shape of dinosaurs and pachyderms, of a brontosaurus and a mother elephant leading a child by her tail.

There is the Viña del Mar Municipal Band that has existed for generations. Composed of a dozen or so gentleman who stand in their tan suits and ties, they deliver songs for parkgoers' consumption and pleasure every weekend.

Yet as wondrous as all of these treasures may be, they all pale when compared to the nimble feet and unquenchable thirst for performance of Edmundo Verdugo Carnitas.

Edmundo is a natty dresser with a red bow tie and sweater, a white scarf that matches the feather in his black bowler cap and a long black jacket. He's got a Chaplinesque mustache, plenty of white stubble, few, if any, teeth and an unblinking gaze.

He's also 97 years old.

We met when he was standing near the band during a lull in performance. He rested part of his weight on his cane.

We talked long enough for me to establish his name and age. I started to ask him another question, but then the music began.

Edmundo stepped forward and started dancing, shedding decades by the second.

His tongue protruding the way basketball legend Michael Jordan's used to wag as he took flight, he moved forward and back in perfect rhythm, twirled in a circle, put his cane through his legs twice, spun it around and caught it cleanly.

Edmundo's awareness that I was taking pictures of him only heightened his energy. Off came the bowler hat in a salute to the crowd of about a dozen people—a move that revealed an impressively full head of hair.

One more spin of the cane.

Edmundo didn't catch it, but his feet still kept time as he bent to pick it up.

The glitch didn't dampen the audience's enthusiasm. They applauded vigorously after the song ended.

I asked Edmundo to write down his name, which he did in shaky but legible letters.

Dunreith and I started walking toward the paths, but looked back as the band struck up their version of *Tequila*, complete with chanting the word at the right moments in the song.

Edmundo was still dancing.

We only stayed in Viña for about half a day, so we know we'll return to see the rest of what it has to offer.

I know where I'm going.

Bar Liguria
and the Power of Place

Posted on August 2, 2013

Eduardo Riveros demonstrates augmented reality at Bar Liguria.
(Photo courtesy of Jeff Kelly Lowenstein)

Some bars just have it.

That combination of noise and brightness and darkness and alcohol and food and colors and smells and seats and music that just allows you to relax, engage in stimulating and expansive conversation, and, on a basic level, be who you truly are.

Here in Santiago, the Bar Liguria near the Manuel Montt Metro station is one of those places.

I've been there twice in the past three evenings. Even though the company was different both times, I emerged with a similar uplifted feeling.

On Tuesday I met with Eduardo Riveros, founder and head of VisionBionica.com, and his friend Geishy Rondón.

Eduardo and I had connected at last week's Data Tuesday at the Movistar Innova space further south on Providencia Avenue.

He had told me about his work with augmented reality, a technology that allows him or whoever else who uses it to essentially embed additional images, video or a web site on a print page.

Short and energetic, Eduardo has a high-pitched laugh and moves his hands in decisive motions. He had prepared a sample page from an award-winning *Chicago Tribune* project friends and colleagues Gary Marx, Alex Richards and David Jackson did last year about school truancy in the city

Eduardo pointed his phone at the page.

Three circles swirled on the phone's face. Then the options appeared.

One was Gary's Twitter account so that people who enjoyed the article could then write a Tweet or send a direct message to Gary.

The second was a video with Diane Sawyer about the Chicago Public Schools' teacher strike last fall.

And the third was a YouTube video of an irate student berating a teacher and walking out of the classroom.

All available for consumption.

Eduardo explained that he had developed a tourism site for Santiago where, while you were in one place, you could point your phone at that landmark and a bunch of other sights to see in the city would appear.

I asked Eduardo what had prompted him to go into this area of work.

He explained that he's Chilean with Venezuelan roots and had just spent a decade in Chavezlandia, much of it going between Barinas y Cumaná.

Although he enjoyed the people and has many warm memories of his time there, the country's relentless violence hit him directly. Two friends were killed, and he had a gun pointed at his neck. The last experience prompted Eduardo to get out of on-the-street reporting and into learning how to tell stories through augmented reality and other means.

His journey led him to earn a Master´s degree in Communication from the University of Havana—Castro's Cuba and Chávez's Venezuela had many cultural, academic and social exchanges—to gain certification from Junaio, a German company that he said is considered the top in the world, and to take online courses from Stanford.

Eduardo had also invited Geishy, a friend who had just earned a diploma in Chile and found work at the Telethon.

Geishy explained that while she had not been a victim of violence in her native Venezuela, the pervasiveness of it and the volume of incidents she witnessed and walked by were such that she wants to stay here rather than return to her homeland.

Huddled around the sturdy wooden tables, we leaned in to hear each other over the steady rumble of other customers. In addition to their work, we talked about the political situation in Venezuela and the seismic difference in charisma between the late Hugo Chávez and Nicolás Maduro, his comparatively pedestrian successor.

If Tuesday night's conversation focused on work, social violence and politics, Thursday evening was like a river with many dips and bends that flowed fast and wide.

In addition to Dunreith, fellow Fulbrighter Stephen Sadlier, Gonzalo Salazar and his lovely wife Jacqui, a Brit, joined us.

We met Gonzalo and Jacqui last week at the civil registry, where we were going through distinct yet related Chilean bureaucratic challenges. Gonzalo, who was born in Chile to a wealthy family, has a British and Chilean passport. The Chilean one has expired, yet he explained that this is the only country in the world in which he is considered Chilean. As a result, if he left the country, he'd not be permitted back in because of his expired passport.

Like Steve, Dunreith and I were trying to have our visa be successfully entered at the civil registry.

Like him, we had had each finger and thumb dipped in black ink.

Like him, we were told that the stamp the Chilean authority put on our passport was not legible.

We prevailed upon the woman, perhaps the same one Steve has encountered in his visits, to not have us go back to the federal police station where we had been the day before.

She consented, but she told us we had to check online to make sure the task was completed by August 8, adding that we would have to start all over again if it was not. I ran out to the gate to go to the store around the corner to make an additional copy of the document the women said she needed.

On Thursday night, though, administrative difficulties were the last topic on the proverbial table for discussion. We also took a deep dive into family history—Steve comes from Haitian Creole and Catalonian stock, while Gonzalo can trace his roots back to the eighth century with documents and talked about an ancestor who fathered 120 children—before tackling national and regional levels of self-esteem in Chile and the United States.

Steve asserted that Americans are fascinated with death and being victims.

Together, we talked about some of the major items Chile has exported to the rest of Latin America and the world: a roster of poets that extends deep beyond Gabriela Mistral and Pablo Neruda; Mistral's progressive educational vision; and the Chicago Boys' model of economic stabilization and a certain technocratic sensibility.

Whereas Tuesday I had a rich stout, on Thursday we had a strong pisco sour and the first carmenere wine I've ever drunk to accompany a plate of goat cheese and macha a la parmesana.

Thursday night also saw a band of older men playing traditional Chilean folk music, along with the theme from *The Godfather*, at a volume that made it increasingly difficult to hear each other.

We kept talking, though.

The truth is that I don't know either how often I'll see Eduardo, Geishy, Gonzalo, Jacqui or Steve again, or how deep the ties will go if we do.

But what eventually becomes of our relationships is not the point.

Rather it's that in a period of transition, at different stages of our lives, from countries around the globe, we met, we drank, and we shared time that was both memorable and invigorating.

Bar Liguria's welcoming environment helped make that happen.

We'll be back.

Maria Eliana and Humberto's Many Gifts

Posted on August 6, 2013

Maria Eliana and Humberto before heading to their house.
(Photo courtesy of Jeff Kelly Lowenstein)

Maria Eliana Eberhard and her husband Humberto gave us many gifts during our leisurely, languidly unfolding nine-hour afternoon and evening of eating, drinking, talking and driving on Saturday.

They gave us unhurried time and unselfconscious generosity.

They introduced us to their new friend David Rojas and his lovely wife Maria Luz, whom they had met during a month-long tour of Eastern Europe headed by a former priest from Spain named Faustino.

They took us to our first vineyard in Chile, the venerable Santa Rita vineyard founded by Don Domingo Fernández Concha in 1880 that has continued to grow and expand in the ensuing 130 years.

They gave us the gift of a delicious lunch in a long, cool dining hall of a hacienda with high ceilings and a red stucco roof.

We missed the 3:00 p.m. tour by a full two hours, but we got plenty of education.

As with friend and colleague Alejandra Matus, Dunreith and I were treated to a virtual seminar in Chilean history during the past four decades.

We covered the key role José Toribio Merino played in the 1973 coup, the current presidential contest between Evelyn Matthei and Michelle Bachelet, the impact Pinochet had on the nation, whether they voted Si or No in 1988 to end Pinochet's reign and the legacy of the Chicago Boys for the country.

The talk wasn't all political.

Maria Eliana and Humberto shared humorous travel misadventures in Mexico and England, while David´s face glowed with pleasure as he talked about two of his three sons working with him in the same clinic where they are all neurosurgeons.

They talked about Chile's emergence from a more isolated and less self-confident nation to one whose people are more assertive and forthright. (At the same time, they made it abundantly clear that whatever gains in self-confidence have been made, the levels they demonstrate still pale in front of those exhibited by many Argentinians.)

Everyone laughed when I followed by suggesting that Dunreith has an Argentinian heart.

They welcomed us into their home and offered "the elevens", an expanded version of tea time, complete with more than a dozen tea choices, mashed avocado that looked like guacamole, ham and crunchy wheat bread in small, circular slices.

Humberto shared his passion for music, his face expanding with joy as he talked about Arthur Rubinstein´s virtuosity and played for us a recording that evokes a smaller Moldovan river merging into the larger, crashing body of water, the music rising in a crescendo as the piece progresses.

Yet the biggest gift in all the extraordinary generosity they showed us was not about Chile.

It was about my father, a cardiac anesthetist at Massachusetts General Hospital and a professor at Harvard Medical School.

In 1984, Maria Eliana and Humberto packed up their belongings and their two young boys, took the money they had saved and the nanny they had hired, and moved to Boston for a year for training in their respective medical professions. (Maria Eliana is an anesthetist, while Humberto is a cardiologist.)

Maria Eliana worked in the laboratory of Warren Zapol, one of Dad's closest friends.

Humberto did not work with Dad, but talked about meeting him.

"Did your father have a small office?" he asked.

I said that he did.

Humberto described how he had entered the area before Dad's office and seen his two secretaries, the notoriously straight-laced Ilse Kaprelian, a German woman who was married to an Armenian motorcycle rider named Gil, and the wisecracking Louise Hotz.

Humberto explained that he felt intimidated for a number of reasons.

He was not in the same field as Dad.

His English was limited.

And Dad was a professor.

With trepidation he opened the door. What he saw astounded him.

There were papers and books everywhere, stretching all the way up to the ceiling.

On the desk.

On the couches.

On the seats.

Then he met Dad, who had apparently just come from the operating room. Humberto knew this because Dad was wearing a puffy blue hat that Humberto was more accustomed to seeing on the head of a Chilean woman.

This was the professor, he wondered?

Dunreith told the table that, before he left Massachusetts General Hospital, Dad was given stationary with a cartoon version of a glasses-wearing Dad being buried in a sea of paper over the words, "From the desk of Ed Lowenstein."

But then Humberto talked about how friendly and down-to-earth Dad was, how he treated him with dignity and respect and welcomed him into the community of doctors at one of the world's most prestigious hospitals.

Maria Eliana echoed the same sentiments.

I've come to learn in life that the family that we know in our homes is only a part of them, and, more than that, that we leave parts of ourselves with people with whom we interact and share meaningful moments.

Although the time has long since passed since I have hungered to really know Dad, that was indeed the case for many years. One of the greatest benefits of working in his laboratory for two summers during college was that it gave me an opportunity to see how he was at work and what he meant to the people there.

"Your dad's a regular guy like us," my colleagues would say quietly. "He's not like a lot of those other doctors who think they're better than us."

"He takes public transportation," another told me.

One man, a Hungarian immigrant, told me about how Dad stuck up for him when he was working on an experiment and a doctor said that he was doing it wrong. Your father said, "Joe is right," the man told me, his stocky body suffused with gratitude.

Nearly 30 years after I worked in the blood gas lab, I have a better sense both of the impressiveness of Dad's accomplishments as well as the importance of what he gave to Humberto and Maria Eliana.

Dad came to the United States after fleeing Nazi Germany on a program called the Kindertransport, I told the group. He never forgot what it was like to be a refugee in a new and unfamiliar country.

The conversation passed and we moved on to five more hours of the marathon visit.

But the gift of letting me know my father in just a slightly different way remained.

The End of Basque Week at the Estadio Español

Posted on August 7, 2013

Hilda and Amador, who have been married for 68 years, at the Estadio Español.
(Photo courtesy of Jeff Kelly Lowenstein)

"Love and the truth," Gonzalo Salazar's mother Hilda declared. "That's the basis for marriage."

She would know.

She and her husband Amador have been married for 68 years, and together for 70.

Hilda is 88 years old, but looks at least a decade younger, the product of a lifetime of tennis, healthy living and a love of dance that surfaced when she heard the strains of traditional Basque music.

We were sitting at the table set aside for the family for the final event of Basque Week at Santiago's Estadio Español, the city's social club for Santiago residents with Spanish ancestry.

Dunreith and I had visited the grounds our first week in the city with friends Miguel Huerta, Macarena Rodriguez and their sons Martín and Domingo, but it was near sundown so I didn't have a sense of all that the facility had to offer.

This time, I was there with Gonzalo, whose parents were among the club's founders shortly after World War II by Spanish émigrés, and his wife Jacqui.

During a leisurely stroll along the idyllic settings and acres of grounds, Gonzalo explained to me the difference had been there when he was a boy more than six decades ago—he's now 67—and what it has now.

The growth has been exponential.

There's a garden for children and many more sports facilities that are used by people from at least three generations Prime red clay tennis courts. An astroturf soccer field for men and a grass space for the youth.

A mini-golf course where dozen of players in full golf outfits were waiting their turn to play one of three holes that at most were 30 yards away. Indoor basketball and an outdoor bocce ball courts. Places for the Spanish version of racquetball. A clear blue swimming pool surrounded by a walkway with arches and a view of the Andes.

As we approached the banquet hall, I asked Gonzalo whether political divisions and exile politics still exist within the community, similar to those among Iranian émigrés. Chuckling, he explained those tensions, along with the attachment to Spain, have diminished with each successive generation.

But what has not decreased is the huge volume of social energy at the club.

Of the more than 4,000 families that belong to the club, close to half live in about a four-block radius, many in a building that resembles a ship and that stands directly outside the grounds.

Gonzalo saw his high school chemistry teacher, a former priest named Luis Fernando who left the ministry, married and is now a grandfather. They hugged and caught up briefly with each other.

We walked by a man with long, dark hair in a ponytail and beard who was wearing a red beret and playing a Basque horn that looked liked their equivalent of a Shofar, a ram's horn used in the Jewish tradition on Yom Kippur, our Day of Atonement. Thin intertwined green, red and white string dangled from the instrument.

We entered a long, chilly banquet hall, checked in with a pair of elderly men and found our table, which had a white tablecloth with a bright red cloth strip laid across the middle. The chairs alternated between white cloth and white with a red sash tied midway around them. Each neatly set plate had a primer on basic Basque vocabulary translated from the Spanish.

Hello was "Kaixo".

Wine was "Ardo".

Lunch was "Bazkari".

We were at Table 18 toward the back of the room.

Hilda got there first, looking dazzling in a black pants suit that matched her hair and a black and white scarf.

Clad in a dark jacket, tan sweater, and a red tie tied in a thick knot, his black beret tilted to the right, Amador came later, accompanied by Gonzalo's brother Tito and his family. Another cousin and his wife from Peru joined us, too.

I told Hilda how I had heard about her, but had trouble believing that she was indeed 88 years old.

She affirmed that she was, and, shortly afterward, took out from her wallet a black and white picture of herself in a bathing suit as the teenaged woman her husband fell in love with 70 years ago.

"I knew right away that he was the man of my life," she said.

Then came a photo of a serious-looking Gonzalo at age seven, getting ready to dance with his older sister, followed by an image of Gonzalo's brother as a baby in a carriage next to a dark haired mother and father.

Cultural entertainment appeared in between the courses. A boy, wearing a red beret and scarf, his right index finger pointed upward and holding his smartphone in his left hand, initiated the ceremony with a burst of high-pitched Euskadi.

Four young women dressed in white hats, black vests and aprons, and red dresses with black stripes stood on the stage at the front of the room, their skirts whirling as they snapped, stepped and jumped the traditional dances to the accompaniment of recorded Basque music.

There was also a Basque version of the Conga line, dancing in which Gonzalo participated, and a series of raffle prizes.

Tito instructed us to concentrate hard on the Number 18 when our table wasn't winning, and eventually the strategy worked. Jacqui's seat was called and she marched happily up to the front of the room to collect her prize.

The last of the gifts were announced and the crowd started to dwindle.

We made plans to get together again soon, possibly at a fish restaurant, and I headed back to our apartment to meet Dunreith.

As I walked to the El, thoughts about traditions altered, but not broken, over time and generations and about the communities within a community jumped around in my head.

But mostly I thought about the love between Gonzalo's parents, that his mother knew instantly and in her core would be forever, and that has proven to be so, through up and downs, children and grandchildren and great-grandchildren, and continues undimmed, even as they near the end of their lives.

A photograph of a young Hilda that she shared at the Estadio Español.
(Photo courtesy of Jeff Kelly Lowenstein)

Meeting Dr. Juan Zuchel at Cerro San Cristóbal

Posted on August 17, 2013

Juan Zuchel, man of many talents and even more information.
(Photo courtesy of Jeff Kelly Lowenstein)

If there's one thing Dunreith and I have learned in our first five weeks here in Chile, it's that there are no end of places to meet people.

I met augmented reality ace and entrepreneur Eduardo Riveros at last month's Data Tuesday, held at innovation space Movistar Innova.

I met Juan, a nine-year-old Colombian boy who had moved here four months ago with his mother, at the Federal Police Station in downtown Santiago.

I met Gonzalo and Jacqui Salazar while trying to get out of the civil registry compound to get a copy made of a page that the female bureaucrat said was unclearly written.

And, today, we met doctor, author, half-marathoner, two-time husband, father, grandfather, great-grandfather and Concepción loyalist Juan Zuchel close to the summit of Cerro San Cristóbal.

We were on a quest to make the four-mile trek so that we could approach, and even touch, the massive white statue of the Virgin Mary.

It's not that I'm suddenly considering becoming Catholic. Rather, it's that we can see the statue from the balcony where we've already been treated to all manner of gorgeous sunsets. On Thursday night, during a pleasant evening with several Santiago-based Fulbrighters, we learned from two of them who jog daily up to the top that it's a very pleasant run and an accessible trail and decided to check it out for ourselves.

By the time we met Juan, we had already passed a determined group of red-jacketed and red-shirted striking postal workers gathered at Pio Nono, a major Santiago intersection that leads into the funky Bellavista neighborhood that's heavy on Lapis Lazuli shops and student eating and drinking options. (The University of Chile is right nearby.)

A number of workers appeared to have slept in tents next to the Rio Mapocho.

According to the *Santiago Times*:

> *The workers are asking postal service Correos de Chile—*
> *an autonomous state enterprise—for a 50,000 peso (US$97) raise*
> *per month. This figure was negotiated two years ago, according to*
> *Jessica Havia, the secretary of the National Postal Workers Syndicate*
> *(SOP). Already irritated over the delay in payment, new raises for*
> *managerial staff pushed workers to strike.*

But if the workers were irritated, they certainly didn't show it.

Like yesterday, they were chanting, singing, blowing whistles and horns and seeking to collect money from passersby in an effort to keep going as the strike extended to the end of its second week.

Dunreith and I walked to the left of the park where we had been our first weekend in Chile and started our trek up the mountain. We had plenty of company.

A stream of walkers, bikers, bike-walking bikers, joggers, and cars also made their way toward the summit.

Although it's still winter, the temperatures stretched upward of 75 degrees. As is often the case, Dunreith had more foresight than me and put on sun block.

But, though we brought a dozen tiny clementines that Dunreith had purchased yesterday at the Tirso de Molina market, neither of us had brought water. This omission started to take its toll as we wound our way around the sun-exposed asphalt surface.

The air got clearer as we rose in altitude. We were increasingly able to see the smog that hangs over the city like a cloud and that seems, almost magically, to work its way into our two-room apartment at rates that require twice, if not thrice, daily, cleanings.

Beyond the smog, we were also able to see the snow-capped Andes. I took a series of pictures using the panorama feature, including one that also featured the multi-story gleaming glass cell phone building.

Enter Dr. Zuchel, who was coming down the mountain.

Clad in a blue t-shirt with a red Z inside a yellow triangular shape over his heart, he had a ring of sweat around his neck. He looked younger than his 68-years, had sturdy legs which had propelled him to a second-place finish in his age group during last year's Santiago half-marathon, and, we learned a little later, a nearly hairless chest.

"I call this a monument to consumerism," he told us.

This was not the first critical comment we had heard about the structure.

During our first week in Santiago, Alejandra Fritz, our uber-guide at Pablo Neruda's house La Chascona, fired a salvo against it, too.

"It was fortunate that Don Pablo did not live to see this built because he would have had a direct view from his home and would not have liked it," she said.

For Juan, the anti-cellphone tower statement was only the beginning of his conversational gambit.

In short order, he informed us that he was from Concepción and that he was both a surgeon and a forensic doctor who taught at the University of Concepción, the most beautiful university in the land. (Here he dipped his head to show us the university's name on his yellow hat.)

Juan also told us that he had a German father and Chilean mother, but could only speak a little German. He has four daughters and one son from his first wife and two daughters from his second one. He has seven grandchildren and one great-grandchild. One of the children is a doctor, while two others are psychologists, he told us after urging us to walk with him toward the summit.

Juan also let us know that he has written seven books about everything from love to children's literature, that the entire area of Concepción would support Michelle Bachelet, the former president who is currently seeking re-election, and that the pediatrician and former torture survivor would earn a decisive victory in November.

"I also suffered under Pinochet," he told me as we continued walking closer and closer to the top. When I asked him for more details, he said that he had been detained repeatedly, but not tortured.

"I can't lie," he said.

I told Juan that I hadn't known how divided the country still was about the Pinochet era, adding that I had spoken with many people who offered freely their opinions that life was more orderly, respectful and generally better during the dictatorship than in the 23 years since he left power in 1990.

"It all depends on your circle and how much it affected you," he answered.

The conversation was flowing easily and the increasing presence of tourist wares told us that the summit was getting closer and closer.

But, amidst all of Juan's sharing, one part confused me; he kept telling us that he was looking for his green family car.

"It's got to be somewhere," he told me early in our conversation.

Where exactly that somewhere would be was not clear to me.

There appeared to be both no car that color anywhere in sight as well as absolutely no room in either lane for said car to park, if indeed it actually existed.

Juan kept referring to the car throughout our conversation and trek upward, which lasted about 20 minutes.

I found myself torn between wondering if his car was the Chilean version of Mr. Snuffleupagus, the "imaginary friend" from *Sesame Street*, or if this was the entry point to some request for us to lend him money to get down to the bottom of the mountain on a funicular. We arrived at the top.

Juan waved us through the gates and told us he would meet us inside since he had to wait for the auto.

We smiled, inwardly shook our heads, and gratefully gulped down the water, Gatorade and reheated mushroom and cheese empanada we bought from a stand near the end of a row. We walked up dozens of cobbled steps toward the massive white statue of the Virgin Mary, her arms uplifted to the heavens.

Like I do when I reach the halfway point of lengthy runs, I felt compelled to touch the structure before we turned to start making our way back down the mountain.

We walked past rows of neatly manicured and multicolored flowers as the strains of solemn religious music washed through the air.

Dunreith, who had just had a small bite of the empanada, brightened when she saw a stand where she could buy ice cream.

His back turned to us, Juan was standing there with a young girl with straight, blond hair.

He had shed the hat and was wearing a white t-shirt that declared his allegiance to the band Los Jaivas, a group whose members have mixed rock with South American ancestral music for the past half-century. (Juan had said he'd just seen one of their concerts the night before.)

After a quick consultation with Dunreith, I tapped him on the shoulder.

Juan turned. His eyes gleamed when he saw us.

"This is my youngest daughter," he said. "I met my family."

So he had.

They were there, sitting on the brick ledge that lined the steps across from the ice cream shop.

His wife Valeska and second-youngest daughter Francisca. His cousin Jaime, Jaime's wife Belén, their daughter Alejandra and granddaughter Ximena.

We chatted for a while.

"Did he tell you that he's written books?" Belén asked.

"He did," I replied. "One book for every day of the week. He also told me about being a surgeon and forensic doctor, about running 10 half-marathons and about teaching at the University of Concepción."

"He told you a lot," Valeska said meaningfully, her tone suggesting that her husband's loquaciousness was an occasional, if not frequent, source of irritation for her.

"I talk a lot, but I don't say much," I responded, then laughed much harder than anyone else in the group.

We moved on to other topics, like whether Francisca had a boyfriend (she did), and whether Alejandra might be interested in my brother Jon (she appeared intrigued, but Jon's never having been married at 43, and, perhaps more important, the thousands of miles between their homes seemed to present a prohibitive barrier for her).

The conversation was just at the point when it could have started to expand and go in all kinds of directions when Juan intervened.

"Let's go to the Virgin," he said.

His family rose as if they were a single person.

We hugged and kissed each other.

Before the family departed, I asked all of them to write their names down so that I could remember them. More hugs and kisses, and the family started walking to their destination. Dunreith and I turned to go, but, before we did, I read the names.

"We'll wait for you in Concepción!" Francisca had written in large blue letters, an exclamation point with a strong line emphasizing the end of the sentence.

I don't know if we'll go to Chile's largest city, or, if we do, whether we'll see Juan's family.

But I do know that our time here has shown again and again the myriads of people, each of whom has their own unique story and particular desire to connect, that exist in this country, and in the world.

We didn't need to come to Chile to learn this, of course. But somehow being here and new and outsiders and open has allowed us to see this more than usual, and to benefit from the exchanges.

Tomorrow, Dunreith and I will go for a walk, see a museum or explore a new part of Santiago.

I can't wait to see who we meet next.

Speaking about Dr. King and Dr. Bass at St. George's College

Posted on August 19, 2013

Things are starting to groove here in Santiago, and it feels deep down good.

For starters, Dunreith and I have found a favorite, reasonable restaurant, La Republiqueta, a funky joint on Avenida Lyon, right where we stayed when we first arrived. She goes for a quesadilla salad with all kinds of seeds, while I have a sandwich with three kinds of mushroom and cheese. Throw in a mate to feed her burgeoning passion for that drink, a seltzer water for me, and a tip, and we're out of there for less than $25.

From there we've established a firm, if not unbreakable, nightly ritual of splitting a chocolate bar filled with marzipan and a glass of the latest red wine we're sampling during the next episode of the original version of *Betty, La Fea*, the inspiration for the American series, *Ugly Betty*.

A project that I've been working on around the Chicago Boys, the group of young Chilean economists who trained under Nobel Prize-winning economist Milton Friedman at the University of Chicago in the 1970s and applied his theories in Chile, is starting to bear some early fruit.

I'm having a terrific time with my students, who call me either "profe" or "Jeff Kelly," and am starting to connect with more colleagues at the university.

Dunreith is making great strides in Spanish, understanding just about everything and being able to speak more and more.

We've got our travel plans to Argentina and Brazil in October just about salted away.

I've started running again after a three-year hiatus, and my body is holding up well so far.

Dear friends Lisa Cook and Jim Peters will be flying here on Sunday morning for close to a 10-day visit.

And this morning I confirmed a speaking gig at St. George's College, a private, English-language school, for next Wednesday, August 28. Hugo Rojas, a law professor with whom I first connected in 2008 during my second attempt to land a Fulbright, connected me to his wife, a teacher at the school.

As justice-loving people the world over know, this year will mark 50 years since Dr. King gave his historic "I have a dream" speech. Although he had delivered a similar version of the speech earlier in Detroit, King abandoned his notes and delivered an impassioned call for the nation to be true to its founding creed and that one day "the sons of former slaves and the sons of former slaveowners shall eat together at the table of brotherhood". The changed speech is a high point in American oratory and history.

Twenty years ago, good friend Dennis Downey and I, along with our ladies at the time, attended the 30th anniversary march on Washington.

Fifty years ago, personal hero Leon Bass was in the crowd of 250,000 people, weeping as he heard Dr. King describe his prophetic vision for the nation.

I've had the great privilege of knowing Leon for close to 20 years throughout his ceaseless commitment to fighting bigotry by talking for organizations like Facing History and Ourselves and the Anti-Defamation League. Over that time we've become close friends. He attended the second wedding Dunreith and I held at Look Park, giving us a check for $100 and telling me to go see a friend called "Gourmet."

A couple of years ago, after more than a decade of pushing from me and other people who love him, Leon published his autobiography, *Good Enough: One Man's Memoir on the Price of the Dream*. It's a remarkable story that begins in 1925 and continues until today. It's a story of tradition and race and service and family and humility and seeking to find the courage to do the right thing.

Leon takes the reader through his childhood in Philadelphia, where he grew up with four brothers and one sister. His father, whom he revered, was a Pullman porter. His mother ran a proverbial tight ship. As Leon's told thousands of audiences, "If corporal punishment was child abuse, I was abused many times." But he always makes it clear that he knew his parents loved him and wanted the best for him.

After graduating from high school in 1943, Leon volunteered to serve in the army. But he was dismayed, and later furious, to find out that the country he had pledged to serve with his life, if necessary, was treating him as if he wasn't good enough by making him stand at the back of the bus and eat at the back of restaurants.

He survived the Battle of the Bulge before having an experience that, as he described it, brought the blinders off and helped him understand that hatred was not limited to those who detested African-Americans. This occurred in 1945, when he witnessed the liberation of the Buchenwald concentration camp in Germany and saw what he called "the walking dead." Bass spent about four hours in the camp. That time was enough to alter his life's perspective, even if he didn't speak publicly about it for decades.

He returned home from the war and became the first member of his family to go to college, generally, but not always, heeding his father's words to not go running his mouth so that he could complete his education.

"Once you get that, no one can take that away from you," his father said.

Bass eventually graduated, becoming a teacher.

In the mid-50s, after some initial reservations, he became a follower of Dr. King after learning about his endorsement of the discipline and philosophy of non-violence.

One day, King came to Philadelphia, and Bass brought his class to hear him speak.

"He was a little guy," Bass recalled, referring to King's comparatively small stature. "But then he started speaking and I recognized him for the giant of a man that he was."

King's message to the students was direct. "Not all of you may become doctors or lawyers, but whatever you do, you be the best at it. If you have to sweep the streets, so be it," he told them. "You sweep the streets the way Michelangelo painted his paintings."

Bass was mesmerized, and, when the March on Washington came, he made his way down from Philadelphia to hear King offer his soaring rhetoric that endures to this day.

Bass later became a principal at Benjamin Franklin High School, one of the toughest in the city, if not the entire nation. He served there for 14 years before retiring in 1982.

About a decade before that, while at the school, he came across a Holocaust survivor talking to a class in the school. She had lost almost all of her family, but the students were not interested in hearing about her pain.

Bass intervened, and, for the first time since that day in Buchenwald a quarter century earlier, spoke publicly about what he had seen.

"What's she saying is true," he told the young men. "I know because I was there."

After the class ended and the students filed out in silence, the survivor implored Bass to start speaking in public.

"You've got something to say," she said.

He has done it since.

One of my favorite parts of working at Facing History was taking speakers like Leon around to talk with students.

Leon and I traveled with his wife Mary, who was starting to be in the grip of Alzheimer's, to Springfield, where he spoke to the entire student body at Cathedral High School.

I took him to Dorchester High, where, in his mid-70s, he stood down a group of unruly students by telling them, "You want to talk, you can come up here and talk," and then staring hard at them.

And I had the pleasure of working with Leon to tell his story in 20 minutes at a Facing History dinner that honored his years of service to the organization and that included a tribute by Dr. Calvin Morris, my former boss at the Community Renewal Society and one of Leon's former fifth grade students.

Indeed, Dunreith and I later traveled to Cleveland, where Leon was again honored by Dr. Morris. That time, I got to have lunch with a select group of former Philadelphians that included Leon, Dr. Morris and one of Dr. Morris' former students who had been a substitute teacher at Benjamin Franklin the last year Leon was a principal there. (They jokingly told me they'd let me hang around as a token Bostonian.)

Dunreith and I called Leon last night. He sounded a bit tired when he answered the phone, but perked up when he recognized my voice. He had just buried Claude, his last remaining sibling, on Friday.

"I'm the last rung on the totem pole," he told me.

Even though there was mercy in his brother's passing as he had suffered for a number of years, sadness crept into Leon's voice.

We talked about our families and his attendance at Obama's second inauguration, an experience he treasured. Although he's not doing as much travel as he used to, he's still speaking up for justice and still working to build the world that Dr. King described so memorably a half-century ago.

I told him about the speaking opportunity next week at St. George's.

"I'll tell the students about Dr. King," I said. "But I'll tell them about you, too."

A Grey Neruda Day
Visiting Isla Negra

Posted on August 24, 2013

Charo Cofré about to play the guitar at her restaurant near Isla Negra.
(Photo courtesy of Jeff Kelly Lowenstein)

"It's grey, but Neruda loved grey," friend, intrepid journalist and unfathomably generous host Alejandra Matus told us. "It's a Neruda day."

She was talking to Jack Fuller, Dunreith and me.

The four of us were sitting in the lobby of the Hotel Plaza San Francisco waiting for Diego Portales University colleague Patricia Rivera to join us before driving to Isla Negra, Pablo Neruda's largest home and the place in which he spent by far the most time.

Jack's the former editor and publisher of the *Chicago Tribune*, where he won a Pulitzer Prize in 1986 for his editorials on constitutional issues.

Alejandra hosted him throughout the week at the university, a time during which he presented to students, alumni and colleagues about his latest book.

Although he's a long-time and accomplished novelist—he told me during the day that he was writing fiction during his training in 1968 in Fort Bragg, North Carolina—his most recent work is about journalism and the challenges that news organizations face in trying to retain large number of readers.

Dunreith and I attended his first presentation, an address on Tuesday evening in which he explained the impact of research about brain activity and the critical role emotion plays in attracting and retaining people's attention.

A central part of his message was that journalists and news outlets need to focus both on retaining standards of journalistic integrity while at the same time integrating new methods based on the knowledge gleaned from the most recent neurological research.

Patricia arrived, we filed into the gray van that matched the day and started the 90-minute ride to Isla Negra.

The Ride and *The Black Book of Chilean Justice*

Relieved of driving and navigational responsibilities, we settled into an easy and amiable conversational flow as we made our way through the rolling green hills.

We moved from the joys and challenges of child rearing in the United States and Chile to Jack's encounters with some of the more Joseph Heller-like moments while serving as a correspondent in Vietnam in 1968, I related to my father's quip, when asked by a colonel why he was wearing his army-issued hat backward, that he wanted people of lower rank to be able to salute him coming and going.

The discussion went in a deeper direction when, at Jack's request, Alejandra told us the story behind, and the response to, *The Black Book of Chilean Justice*, her expose of the corruption and lack of independence in the Chilean judiciary during the Pinochet era.

Investigative stalwart Mónica González invited Alejandra in the early 90s to participate in the project after the publication of a federal report that criticized the judiciary. (González, who now directs CIPER, Chile's strongest investigative publication, later backed out due to other work responsibilities.) Alejandra smiled as she remembered asking her then-editor for two extra weeks of vacation to write the book. He laughed, told her to take the two weeks of vacation and then get to work.

It ended up taking six years.

The book's publication in early 1999 came months after Pinochet's arrest in London in October 1998. The timing was such that the book publishers thought that there would not be a strong official response to the book becoming available nine years after Pinochet left power.

They were wrong.

Drastically so.

Judge Rafael Huerta Bustos ordered all copies of the books confiscated the day after it was published. Chief Justice Servando Jordan invoked the State Security Law, which made it a crime to disrespect public officials or governmental agencies. Among other elements in the suit, he cited the book's cover, which showed three monkeys representing the philosophy of "See-no-evil, hear-no-evil, speak-no-evil."

Alejandra faced five years in prison. Her initial plan was to stay and fight, but three conversations changed her mind.

She spoke with her brother, a lawyer who said she could indeed be imprisoned.

Her publisher said the house couldn't protect her.

And her fiancé looked terrified.

Alejandra decided to flee the country as soon as possible. She flew to Buenos Aires and thought the whole situation would calm down in about 10 days. She didn't return to her country for two-and-a-half years.

A lot happened during that time.

Presidential candidate and later victor Ricardo Lagos made the law and Alejandra's return an issue in his campaign. Tens of thousands of copies of the book were sold on the black market.

La Tercera, Chile's second-largest newspaper, published the book on its website outside of the United States.

Alejandra won a case she filed against the Chilean state in the Inter-American Commission on Human Rights, and received reparations. The law eventually was overturned.

"This is a remarkable story," Jack said.

Patti agreed, adding that many people in Chile consider Alejandra a hero.

The impact of Alejandra's story was soaking in when we pulled off the highway and started driving the final kilometers to Isla Negra.

Isla Negra

We walked around the property and headed down to the beach.

"I came back from my voyages and navigated constructing happiness," was carved in Neruda's distinctive cursive writing into a brown wooden beam holding up the front entrance to the long house that snaked along his property.

Constructing was indeed the perfect word.

Dunreith and I had already seen La Chascona and La Sebastiana, Neruda's homes in Santiago and Valparaíso, so we were prepared for the way Neruda built a world out of his home, his travels, his politics, his writing, his women, and his friends.

We felt ready to see the fantastic objects like a life-size horse made in part of papier-mache and statues of bare-breasted women that Neruda treated as if they were alive, the secret space of the kitchen, a place Neruda considered magical, the sacred sanctuary where he wrote, and the items he acquired from all parts of the planet. (This house contains extensive collections of pipes, bottles, sombreros, butterflies and clam shells.)

We were familiar with Neruda's love of the sea, his penchant for naming houses and friends' books, and his insistence on a robust and well-stocked bar.

But whereas the other homes had a more vertical feel—they were a minimum of four stories each—Isla Negra was defined by its comparative flatness and its clear and stunning views at nearly all points of the house of the Pacific Ocean.

This included the tomb outside where he and Matilde Urrutia, his third and final wife, were buried.

Waves crashed into the rocks in their ceaseless, eternal rhythm, spraying foam high into the air and providing an undulating, calming background accompaniment to the couple's permanent resting place.

Charo Cofré

It was close to 1:00 p.m., and we were all feeling hungry.

Fortunately, Alejandra had arranged for us to eat at a nearby hostel owned by Chilean acoustic guitar legend Charo Cofré. She and her husband

Hugo Arévalo were close friends of Neruda and lived with him for two months in Paris.

A gallery of black and white photographs, several of which were autographed by the poet, and nearly all of which had relevant quotes from his writing pasted onto them, stood along the walls.

Images of Neruda's mother, who died shortly after he was born.

Pictures of the artist in exile, looking like an earlier version of James Gandolfini's Tony Soprano.

A somber shot of the crowd of people, with Hugo identified in the back, who marched to bury Neruda after his death in the first public protest after the coup.

A photograph of his message, written in 1971 in his trademark cursive script, "I am too happy to write. I have to eat and drink with you, dear friends."

We were the only customers in the house.

Well, besides Don Pablo.

A lifelike model of the poet, dressed smartly in a tweed jacket, a red scarf poking out of his white button-down shirt and one of his many hats, sat in the corner.

Dunreith and Don Pablo.
(Photo courtesy of Jeff Kelly Lowenstein)

We all took some pictures next to Neruda, whose fingers moved as if ready to write some more when we started to move away from him. We started the meal with the Chilean standards of a pisco sour and rolls topped with pevre, a salsa equivalent.

Dunreith and I followed Alejandra's lead and ordered caldillo de congrio, a fish soup that was Neruda's favorite dish.

We were well into our meal and a few glasses of white wine when Charo entered, guitar in hand and sat at the head of the table.

Her black haired pulled back tightly against her head, Charo was draped in a green shawl that covered most of her body like a cloak. The color of her light-blue flowered shirt matched her eyeshadow.

Although she regularly performs for hundreds, if not thousands of people, today it was just the five of us.

"I am doing this for Alejandra," she said.

Charo sang about her country, the sea that Neruda loved so deeply and, in a new song, about her mother's hands. Her own hands danced and strummed and plucked as she sang, often with her eyes closed. In between the songs, she told us about Neruda and Matilde.

"People on the left want to say that he was killed by the government, but I think he died of a broken heart," she said. (Neruda passed away just 12 days after the Pinochet coup and subsequent ransacking of La Chascona by military authorities.)

Charo based her opinion on having talked with Matilde regularly in the dozen years after her husband died, a period during which she never mentioned a murder.

Charo told us about shopping at a flea market in Paris for a bottle to add to Neruda's collection. It was no easy task, as he already owned many of the ones they brought to him. But, eventually, they met with success. Neruda rewarded himself with an artery-clogging croque monsieur, a ham and cheese sandwich that he said had to be kept quiet from Matilde.

Charo also talked about how she learned from the joy her mother took in daily life, in small moments like watching tiny chickens move.

Indeed, she said that she had recently told a very wealthy friend that she felt richer than her because of the attitude she has toward her life.

After about half an hour of singing and talking and laughing, Charo said she had to go.

Soon, we did, too, to get Jack to the airport.

The Return

The ride back to Santiago was slower.

Dunreith closed her eyes in the front.

I talked mostly in Spanish with Patti, a documentary film maker and a doctoral student who is doing her dissertation about narrative construction in blogs. Jack and Alejandra discussed the 1976 murder by Chilean government officers of former Chilean ambassador to the United States Orlando Letelier.

We dropped Jack at the airport so that he could catch his return flight home before the driver dropped us at Diego Portales University.

We went with Alejandra to pick up Alejandro, her five-year-old son, and then to meet her husband Alberto, a former militant and exile who is now a political consultant. He hugged and his wife and son. He and his partner were working with Ricardo Yarzo, a candidate for a council position in the upcoming November elections. He's one of 40 candidates seeking to win the eight positions that are available in Punta Arenas, one of the country's southern-most communities.

Alberto introduced Alejandra to Ricardo.

"Do you know her?" he asked quietly, pride seeping through his voice. "She wrote *The Black Book of Chilean Justice*."

Ricardo said that he did.

We downloaded the video I shot of Charo singing, and I showed it to Alberto.

He stopped moving and watched, riveted.

"She is beautiful," he declared.

Alejandra was right.

It was a grey Neruda day.

And so much more.

On Sylvia Broder's Courage

Posted on August 25, 2013

Sylvia Broder makes a point during a dinner she hosted at her apartment.
(Photo courtesy of Jeff Kelly Lowenstein)

Our first six weeks here in Santiago have included a seemingly unending stream of glorious lunches and dinners that start late, end later and last anywhere from four to nine hours.

Thanks to friend Marjorie Agosín, colleagues at Diego Portales University, chief among them the remarkable Alejandra Matus, family connections, folks from Chicago and the Fulbright program, we've had the extraordinary good fortune to meet a wide range of fascinating, generous, committed and intelligent people who have opened their homes and hearts to us.

Yet even though our lengthy initial meetings have allowed us to forge connections of a surprising depth, I've also felt an almost inevitable reserve of distance from the folks we've met. It's as if, to draw from the Czech writer Milan Kundera's *The Unbearable Lightness of Being*, we don't yet know if the words we are speaking mean the same thing on each side, or rather if we simply are speaking from a Dictionary of Misunderstood Words.

Now, though, we're starting to see people for a second time, and are finding that the connections are getting deeper.

This was the case yesterday with Sylvia Broder, Marjorie Agosín's cousin who had hosted us and two other couples for a lovely dinner at her apartment in the Vitacura neighborhood the first Thursday after we arrived. She and the couples had previously lived in a property with five houses in Las Condes.

Sylvia and her family were in the middle, flanked on the right and left by each of the friends. The difference was more than geographic. The friends on the left were politically left of center. Jorge Reizin, the husband of the couple who lived on the right, was a self-described extreme right-winger.

During an evening of free-flowing, jazzy conversation, among other topics, we talked about children, and, in Sylvia's case, grandchildren and the vagaries of home repair.

We covered the upcoming presidential election that features Michelle Bachelet and Evelyn Matthei as the two of the nine candidates considered to have the best chance of winning and the complete failure of the Census to arrive at an accurate count. (Jorge advanced the theory that it was a deliberate effort by left-wing bureaucrats to enhance their power in the next government.)

Sylvia also told us about her personal history.

Her mother was a Polish concentration camp survivor, while her father was a Polish partisan who survived the war fighting in the woods like Tuvia Bielski of Defiance fame. Born in post-War Prague, she moved with her family to Chile with her sister at age 10. She did not know that she was Jewish, nor had she yet considered why, as opposed to her classmates, she had no grandparents.

But she did not tell us about the people she hid during the earliest week of the Pinochet dictatorship that took place nearly exactly 40 years ago.

There were two of them.

One she knew. The other she did not.

She hid the one she had not met before in the first week after the coup.

Sylvia had gone to work at the Australian Embassy the morning of September 11, but instantly could tell something serious was happening. She went to a friend's house nearby, but wasn't able to leave for two or three full days.

When she came out, she learned that the man needed help, and took him in without hesitation. She did so, even though her action meant that she could have been detained, tortured or killed. Even more, Sylvia advocated to help the man get out of the country.

The Australian government had not committed itself to an agreement that would have obligated it to take action to assist the man and other victims of the dictatorship, so Sylvia worked with officials of the Canadian government to provide him sanctuary.

Which they did.

Sylvia said she did not consciously think of her family's background, her parents' survival and her murdered relatives whom strangers had not helped, when deciding to take the man who did not speak into her home.

But she's sure it played a role in her decision.

Several weeks later, a friend also needed a refuge. Sylvia let him stay for close to a month. Her neighbor sheltered someone, too. The fugitives hid during the day, and they all enjoyed themselves at night.

Sylvia said there were other neighbors who supported Pinochet and knew what she was doing. But they didn't turn her in. The friend later escaped to Cuba, lived in other countries and eventually returned to his homeland.

Another one of Sylvia's friends, a woman, called to take her to a family event.

After picking us all up downstairs, she took us on a harrowing ride that evoked Woody Allen's ride with Diane Keaton in *Annie Hall*.

We survived and started our walk down Providencia Avenue and past sites like the Fulbright office and Santa Isabel supermarket that have become increasingly familiar during the past six weeks.

As we walked, we were filled with a sense of quiet wonder at Sylvia's unreflecting courage and at our great privilege of learning about the many layers she and others are already starting to reveal as we start to shed our initial interaction of host and guest and begin to relate to each other as fellow journeyers on the road of life.

On Hugo Rojas' Longing for Pisco Sour and Ceviche

Posted on August 29, 2013

Friend, memory scholar and pisco sour lover Hugo Rojas.
(Photo courtesy of Jeff Kelly Lowenstein)

After two years in England, new friend Hugo Rojas started hallucinating about ceviche and pisco sour from his beloved Chilean homeland.

The professor of the sociology of law shared the details of his visions several hours into a thoroughly enjoyable Saturday evening with Dunreith and his lovely wife Angélica in their living room that has a comfortable couch on one side of the room and a neatly ordered bookshelf lined with English and Spanish volumes on the other.

Hugo's revelation came after we had met his nine-year-old daughter Victoria, an avid reader who brought out three hefty, English-language tomes she is working her way through at the moment. Two of the works were by Arthur Ransome, an author who published in the 1940s and whose books Victoria was consuming because she wants to learn about the "old England." Victoria's third book was *The Diary of Anne Frank*.

It came after we had learned about new evidence in a court case being argued in the Chilean Supreme Court at the moment by a friend of his who is positing that former Chilean president Salvador Allende did not, as has been commonly understood, actually commit suicide with a machine gun given to him by Cuban leader and revolutionary comrade Fidel Castro.

Rather, he was murdered, Hugo's friend is asserting.

It arrived after Hugo's telling us about his childhood in Sewell, an American mining town about two hours from Santiago that was nationalized during the Allende era.

His sharing came after he had talked us through the inner workings of Gen. Augusto Pinochet, about Pinochet's middle-class background, insecurity and craving for recognition, and how he was only made aware of the coup that had been planned since November of 1972 on September 9, 1973. Hugo told us about Pinochet's taking a full 30 minutes to sign the document that came just before the coup that signaled he was committed to the plan, yet only did so after signing the document with his own pen and personal seal.

Before Hugo told us about his tantalizing hallucinations, the four of us had consumed most, but not all, of the elegantly garnished seafood—Angélica and Hugo brought out shrimp and salmon and, of course, the ceviche—that we had dished out into individual bowls.

We had moved through drinking a tangy, cold pisco sour to a crispy white wine and a rich red.

The raw emotion of Hugo's statement was in stark contrast with the reserved demeanor he exhibited the first time we met in person several weeks ago for lunch with Dunreith and our mutual friends Miguel Huerta and Macarena Rodriguez, one of Hugo's law school colleagues at the University of Alberto Hurtado.

We had initially connected in 2008, thanks to friend Stacey Platt. After we had exchanged emails and spoken via Skype, Hugo had written a letter of invitation for me to spend a semester at Alberto Hurtado as a Fulbright scholar.

My application was not successful, and we had maintained contact in the ensuing five years.

During our meal together he had talked to me about his dissertation on memory in Chile—when I told him it would be a significant project, he replied, "That's what I keep telling my wife"—his experience of having met Ariel Dorfman in the United States, and his thoughts about why Dorfman is less known and less popular in Chile than fellow émigré author Isabel Allende.

Tall and sturdy, dressed in a sweater and a tweed jacket, his short black hair neatly combed, he exuded intelligence, perspective and reserve.

His statement about his food-based hallucinations contained humor and just a trace of anguish at the memory.

Of course, Hugo is not the first of my foreign-born friends to be driven to intense longing for their native countries.

Ntuthuko Bhengu, a doctor, businessman, and entrepreneur was part of a crew of exchange partner Vukani Cele's friends who hosted me with unstinting generosity throughout my time in Tongaat, South Africa from August 1995 to July 1996.

Like Hugo, Ntuthuko started shuddering as he recalled the bitter winter cold in England that penetrated the core of his being and nearly made him weep with desire for South Africa's fierce humidity and heat.

I had empathy for Hugo, too.

In August 1978, shortly before I was about to join the ranks of Pierce School eighth graders I had wanted to belong since entering kindergarten eight years earlier, Dad had come home and told us that we were moving to Oxford, England for the year.

Academically, it was the hardest of my life, with 12 subjects, school until 12:55 p.m. on Saturday afternoon, and a tracking system that meant, like the English class system, that top marks were allocated for the students in the highest set. This said nothing of teachers who openly mocked our being American and a minister who said that the Jews had had an easy go of things throughout history.

The lowest point for me, the equivalent of Hugo's culinary deprivation and Ntuthuko's winter, was my first midterm report.

In it I received five gammas, the mark that meant I was in the lowest quarter of the class.

I kept my composure during school, and burst into a near inconsolable flood of tears when I got home. I understand what England can do to outsiders.

Angélica, who had arranged for me to speak to students about Dr. King's life and legacy at the St. George's school where she teaches, explained after Hugo spoke that she hates to cook—an announcement that sparked an enthusiastic, sisterly high five from Dunreith.

Nevertheless, she reached within herself to try again and again, perhaps 10 times, to prepare a ceviche that would meet her husband's exacting standards.

Nothing worked.

Angélica was a key figure in a story Hugo told us about a fellow Chilean graduate student also studying in Oxford. A group of the students would gather at each other's homes and share food with each other. This gentleman brought a bottle of pisco sour, but only shared a dollop with each member of the group. When it was time to leave, he looked to take whatever remained in his bottle with him.

"You have to leave it here," Hugo and the others told him.

"No, Angélica told me I could take it," he answered.

"She just told you that because she's a very kind person," the group replied.

The man maintained his insistence on relying on Angélica's kindness, and, eventually left with his bottle. Decades may pass, but the stain on the man's reputation will remain intact among his fellow Chileans.

This March, Hugo, Angélica and their daughters returned to Chile. His mother greeted them when they stepped off the plane. Angélica said Hugo's first words to his mother were, "Mama, did you bring the pisco sour?"

"I have it and the ceviche at home," his mother answered.

The son smiled at the memory of his mother's anticipating, and then meeting, two of his most basic longings.

Hugo and his family have been home for about five months. He's made progress on his dissertation, and has resumed his teaching duties and other responsibilities without difficulty.

He's not hallucinated once about shepherd's pie.

Luis Dreams of a Home in Chillán

Posted on August 30, 2013

Luis has dreamed of the house in Chillán for years.

It's located in the country about four hours away from Santiago, where he grew up and has driven a cab for nearly the past half-century.

He started driving at 19, just after he had legally become an adult and more than a dozen years after both of his parents had died. Luis' father passed away from cancer when he and his twin were just four years old. His mother had a heart attack that same year.

The city has changed a lot since he first got behind the wheel, he told me during a traffic-filled ride to St. George's school on the outskirts of Santiago on Wednesday.

Luis was wearing a blue-striped sweater, a neatly knotted tie, and a shirt with the top button undone. His mustache and the hair on his head were both thick with hefty portions of grey. The topic of the changes in the city since he's been a taxi driver elicited animated hand gestures that evoked his Italian ancestors.

"In the Allende days," he said, "the streets were littered with trash."

"People were drunk all the time. The buildings were all grey. Many people lacked a strong work ethic. Pinochet changed all that," Luis told me.

"People went to bed earlier. They worked harder. In short, Pinochet modernized the city and the country," he said.

Luis has a far dimmer view of politicians these days.

"They're more concerned about serving their own and their parties' interests. They don't think about what the people need," he said.

As a result, Luis said he's not going to vote in the upcoming presidential elections.

But one thing he is sure of, regardless of who wins: the people will have to work like slaves. That includes him.

Which is why he's so excited about his house.

It's in the country, and, in his vision, has got a small goat, a chicken and a rooster. While there, he'll be able to relax and enjoy himself.

Luis doesn't have much family. His marriage with an Arab woman didn't work out. He has two sons in their 30s, neither of whom is married or has children. They've been to Italy, but he's never made it there. His brother's wife died a few years ago.

Still, the image of the home gives him peace as he's chauffeuring customers around the city as many as 80 hours per week.

The problem, though, is money. Luis said he's hardly saved any money in the pension accounts that were established under the leadership of José Piñera, older brother of current Chilean president Sebastián Piñera.

We were pulling up to the front gate at the school.

I waited in the car, gave Luis a tip and wished him luck in converting his vision into a reality.

I asked him for a business card, and he gave me one from the company.

For his sake I hope that, someday soon, Luis will be able to give his final ride to a customer, move south to Chillán and take up residence in the rustic home he's wanted so desperately.

But, as his car rumbled away, I feared instead that Luis may spend the rest of his days and years driving around the city where he has lived his entire life, and from which he is likely never to leave.

Charo Cofré's Many Skills

Posted on August 31, 2013

Charo Cofré's got skills.

Lots of them.

Folk singer.

Activist.

Guardian, along with her husband Hugo Arévalo, of Pablo Neruda's memory.

This morning, Dunreith and I rented a blue Peugeot four-door and drove with dear friends Lisa Cook and Jim Peters to eat, drink and soak in the pleasure of what amounted to a private concert by Charo at Hosteria La Candela, the hostel and restaurant she's run for the past 15 years with Hugo.

Thanks to Alejandra Matus' generosity of including us in a day-long trip with Pulitzer Prize winning-journalist Jack Fuller, Dunreith and I had had the pleasure a week ago Friday of being part of a group of five who were the only people in the spacious room that has a mannequin of Dan Pablo in the corner as well as a spectacular view of the Pacific Ocean crashing onto rocks and spraying foam into wind-swept trees. Charo had played for the five of us at that meal, too, making it clear that she was doing so because she admired and respected Alejandra's work. At the end of our time in the hostel, which has a long gallery of black and white images of Pablo Neruda as well as color shots of Charo with Matilde Urrutia, Neruda's third wife and widow, Dunreith promised her that we would return.

Today, we made good on our promise.

This time, the room was far fuller.

A Chilean couple dined on one side of us, next to a pair of Americans who'd rented a car from the same Sheraton Hotel in Viña del Mar as we had. On the other side of us was a group of about two dozen students from the University of California system who were studying at the University of Chile for a month and were taking a day trip to celebrate the midway point of that time. And a couple of Australians sat across from Don Pablo at the far end of the room.

Hugo, who is lean and compact and whose grey beard matches his full head of hair, came out to prepare the microphone for his wife at around 2:30 p.m.

By that time Dunreith, Lisa, Jim and I had already consumed what has become nearly a daily routine of having a stiff pisco sour, an unofficial Chilean national drink, dolloped some pevre, the Chilean equivalent of salsa, onto a fresh white roll, devoured a fried empanada filled with onions, and made our way through our main courses of shrimp, salmon and my personal favorite, a fish soup that made good on its promise in the menu to leave nothing out.

Charo's entrance only heightened our warm feeling.

She strode to the front of the room, directly in front of the table where we were sitting—our waiter told us that she had chosen that table for us so that we would be able to see her well when she was singing—and, as classic performers do, instantly won the crowd over with her charm, wit and talent.

Her black hair, as it was last week, was pulled back tightly over her head. Her eyebrows and eyeshadow blended perfectly with her hair color.

Whereas last week she was draped in a green shawl that covered most of her body, this time she was wearing a white embroidered tunic with a purple and pink pattern. A long-sleeved purple shirt poked out from the tunic on each arm.

Charo won her first major prize for playing guitar in 1967, and she shows no signs of slowing. After a brief introduction to a Venezuelan instrument known for its four strings, she reached over, picked up another acoustic guitar and started strumming and singing with abandon.

A smile creases Charo's lips as she sings, revealing two full rows of straight white teeth. Her eyes are often closed.

Last time, she sang about her country, the sea that Neruda loved so deeply and, in a new song, about her mother's hands. This time she performed the first two songs, but added other tunes, too.

Alternately fast and slow, soulful and political, they spoke about Neruda's winning the Nobel Prize in Literature for Chile, about her commitment to continue singing no matter what happened in her life, and about a young child whose mother is in the fields.

The crowd was rapt with attention, erupting in applause each time she finished.

All too soon, she completed her final song, raising a full goblet of white wine to the crowd and wishing us all, "Buen provecho."

Enjoy your meal.

We had just wrapped up ours and were starting to walk out of the room and toward Isla Negra, Pablo Neruda's largest and favorite house and where Charo had made a reservation for us.

"I love you, Jeff," she exclaimed in heavily-accented English from her seat in between Don Pablo and the Australian women.

Apparently she was grateful for the blog post I had written about our previous visit. I answered her in Spanish with just enough enthusiasm to elicit a hearty "Hey!" from my wife.

"Oh, right, sorry, honey," I said.

I regained my domestic footing, and Dunreith and I hugged Charo and promised to come back again with Aidan after he arrives in late November.

Along with our dear friends, we set off on the short trip on a sandy road to learn yet again from Don Pablo, fresh memories of our multi-talented hostess following behind us.

September 11 Countdown Begins

Posted on September 1, 2013

Although in theory all days are equal, in truth some matter more than others.

Some dates, like Christmas and Thanksgiving, evoke images of joy and tradition and connection. (Many non-Christians have a different take of the former, while many Native American have a dim view of the latter.) But others days are noteworthy for the memories they stir of pain, suffering and destruction.

In our country, December 7, a day that then-President Franklin Delano Roosevelt called "a date which will live in infamy," is one of those occasions. So, too, is September 11, the anniversary of the terrorist attacks on the World Trade Center and Pentagon.

Here in Chile, September 11 is also a day of major national significance.

For it was on that date in 1973 that the Chilean military, headed by Gen. Augusto Pinochet, ousted democratically-elected Socialist President Salvador Allende and ushered in his 17-year reign.

Diego Portales University Department Chair Carlos Aldunate made the point during a dinner on one of our first weekends in Santiago that Chile has seen similar tensions before in its history. But the memory that resonates loudest in Chile are the echoes from that fateful day. The anniversary matters every year, but this one promises to be particularly important.

The first and most basic reason for this is that a week from Wednesday will mark 40 years since the Pinochet coup. There's something about the passage of a full decade, or decades, that prompts intense revisitation and analysis of key events. (I'm not in the United States at the moment, and can only imagine the frenzy that will build in November around the 50th anniversary of the assassination of 35th President John F. Kennedy.)

The second reason is that November marks the presidential election.

And a third has to do with the personal histories of Michelle Bachelet and Evelyn Matthei, the two major presidential candidates, who have direct ties to the aftermath of the coup. These two highly accomplished women have similar military pasts, but very different political visions for the nation.

In 2006, Bachelet became the nation's first female president. A divorced mother of three children, she served as Defense Minister at the same time that Donald Rumsfeld held that position in the United States. She is also the daughter of a former Chilean Air Force General.

So, too, is Matthei. In many ways, the two women share important similarities besides their fathers' military backgrounds.

The families were close, and the two women were friends as children. Both grew up in privileged homes, attended elite schools, learned to speak multiple foreign languages and took advanced training in a discipline that requires many years to master. (Bachelet is a certified pediatrician, while Matthei is a classically trained pianist.)

It was during the Pinochet era, though, ushered in by the 1973 coup, that the similarities ended.

Whereas Matthei's father was part of the junta, Bachelet's father remained loyal to the constitution and to Allende. Because of that, he was tortured daily at the facility headed by the elder Matthei, even though he personally was not there at the time Bachelet's torture occurred.

Bachelet and her mother both were tortured as well in the infamous Villa Grimaldi compound where legions of others also were tortured, murdered and disappeared. Even though she did not break, Bachelet has said that she still grapples with the emotional scars from that experience.

Bachelet has at different points shown compassion for the torturers, saying they carry bags of guilt with them. When she was elected president, in a gesture of reconciliation, she hugged the elder Matthei and called him "Uncle Fernando."

Yet, in some ways, the most basic reason that the coup's anniversary is such a cultural lightning rod is the basic fact that Chile remains a profoundly divided nation, and memory is at the heart of the divide.

I'll write more about this aspect in the upcoming days.

Tonight, I wanted to signal the deluge of news coverage, television shows, books, conferences, and museum exhibits that have already been published or shown, or will be so during the upcoming week and a half. Sifting through this flood of material will be my focus during the next 10 days.

This includes a week from Wednesday, when the date that bonds Americans and Chileans alike in suffering again occurs for the twelfth and fortieth times since the mornings when history in each country was permanently and irrevocably changed.

Memory at the Heart of a Divided Chile

Posted on September 2, 2013

A picture of three men in blindfolds at the Salvador Allende Museum.
(Photo courtesy of Jeff Kelly Lowenstein)

After seven weeks here and as the fortieth anniversary of the coup led by Gen. Augusto Pinochet draws near, I´ve come to the following conclusion: Chile is a deeply divided country, and memory is at the heart of the divide.

You can see it on the street around the corner from where we live. Close to two months ago, it returned after contentious debate to its original name of Avenida Providencia Norte from Avenida 11 de Septiembre, in honor of the coup that toppled democratically elected Socialist leader Salvador Allende from power. (After giving an emotion-filled speech on Radio Magellanes, the people's radio station, Allende either killed himself with a rifle given to him by Fidel Castro, or was killed, depending on whom you believe.)

You can hear it in the language that Chileans use to describe the 17-year period in which Pinochet held power in the country.

For supporters, it was a period of a military regime.

For opponents, it was the dictatorship.

Carlos Aldunate, journalism department chair at Diego Portales University where I´m teaching, made the point that Chile has had divisions since it gained its independence from Spain. But if historical memory resonates in this land that is close to 3,000 miles long, the noise from the coup is still the loudest.

The buildup to the anniversary is a deluge of panels, films, and programs in radio, broadcast, print and the web, all of which are tackling the question of the fateful time leading up to "el golpe"—the coup—and its aftermath.

You can also see the enduring divisions in *The Judge and the General,* Elizabeth Farnsworth and Patricio Lanfranco's award-winning documentary film about Judge Juan Guzmán. After leaving the insular right-wing world in which he had allowed himself to live, Guzmán immersed himself in the gruesome details of the Pinochet regime, and ultimately indicted the man who had been largely responsible for his professional ascent. The film opens and closes with footage of Pinochet's coffin being carried onto the street after the dictator died without having been prosecuted or convicted of the crimes that impacted so many Chilean families.

Then-President Michelle Bachelet, herself a torture survivor, former exile and the nation's first female president, refused to declare Pinochet's death cause for a national day of mourning. Her decision prompted an outpouring of venomous yelling and epithet-hurling from hundreds, if not thousands, of Pinochet supporters who cursed their newly elected leader and chanted, "They never got him!".

A dismayed Guzmán speaks while watching footage of the protests about the division that clearly existed within the country. "They haven't learned anything," he says.

Of course, Guzmán could have just as easily gained an understanding of the regime's brutality by visiting the *Images of Resistance* Dunreith and I went to at the Salvador Allende Museum on Avenida Republica.

Art at the Salvador Allende museum

A chronology painted on the wall of the room that you enter first explains that Allende established the museum to make art available to and for the people. All of the works in the building, including those by masters like Joan Miró, were donated by the artists.

The chronology signals the importance of the coup by portraying it as a round circle many times larger than the other items on the timeline. Pinochet's seizure of power did not stop the artists who had contributed to the museum and others who joined in the cause from registering their outrage throughout his bloody reign.

The timeline details the years and dates of exhibitions held by artists to show their support of the Chilean people and their opposition to the Pinochet regime. Intellectuals, philosophers and authors like Michel Foucault, Gabriel García Márquez and Roland Barthes also expressed their dissent.

Many of these countries were enduring their own governmental oppression like Poland, Cuba and Mexico. The University of Chile held the work during the dictatorship, showing it again after Pinochet left power in 1990.

The imprint of his reign can be felt throughout the two floors, perhaps nowhere more strongly than in the basement, which the museum calls The Bestiary. The text introducing the room states that the works of art show what happens when the state has unfettered power.

The room contains images of leaders like Pinochet with a Nazi swastika on his sleeve, relentlessly turning flowers into corpses, towering above the landscape he's trampling through. A separate piece is called, *In Nixon We Trust*. Nixon is in the center like a coin. The names of some of his top henchmen who fell in the Watergate scandal—Liddy, Dean, Mitchell, Erlichman and Haldeman—are on the side.

But beyond the political satires there are literally beasts, especially a pair of horrific, grotesque, larger-than-life blue figures, one of which has its own face while the other is a skeleton wearing a mask.

There's also an enormously disturbing image of a small naked man whose buttocks are visible as he lies face down in the stomach of a much larger, reclining Statue of Liberty whose vagina is bleeding profusely.

The second floor shows what The Bestiary wrought.

They did not break us is the title painted in black letters that crawl down the entrance of two of the rooms. But while the inability of the torturers to destroy their victims can arguably be classified as a victory, the pictures in the rooms show the heavy price they paid.

And whereas the basement depicted the depravity of the torturers that was unleashed and given sanction by Pinochet's regime, the second floor generally focuses on the tortured, the murdered, and the survivors.

The first room one enters is drenched in pain caused by the assertion of sheer forcé by the state over its blindfolded citizens.

In one image, three blindfolded men with thick, wavy hair are screaming in anguish. In the next room a man with a gag around his mouth is tied to a pole and forced to bend at his midsection.

Enforced silence is a theme throughout the exhibit. One image has a man´s mouth that looks like part of burlap material that is literally ripped out of the canvas, rendering him mute.

The institutional silence and complicity of *El Mercurio*, the country's leading newspaper for more than a century, is the focal point of the room, Todos Los Poderes, or All the Powers. While guns are a more frequent image in the room and the exhibition as a whole, the dripping blood, paper's name, and resemblance to a distorted front page leave no doubt about the artist´s call for accountability from the paper that consistently went beyond the proverbial turning a blind eye to the regime's abuses to securing, and then publishing, photographs from Pinochet's secret police.

This silence is all the more upsetting in the context of these brutal images.

One of the most haunting painting shows five women in various stages of shame and violation. The perpetrator who presumably abused them is naked. His genitals are visible, but he has no identity above the chest.

The concealing of torturers' identity was a common practice and a theme that runs through a number of the paintings.

In *Interior Room 3*, a two-panel series, another naked woman stands while light is shining on her. She is interrogated by a man wearing sunglasses who appears to be directed by a man speaking into a microphone from the second panel. Behind him a man's carcass lies inside a cage, as if discarded.

After attending an exhibit like this, it seems almost inconceivable that Chileans could somehow think life in the country was better during Pinochet. But Roberto Agosín, a dentist we met in Viña del Mar, said that there are ways for people who want to do so of making sense of such times.

"Whereas Argentina's Dirty War saw 30,000 people killed, in Chile the total was only 3,000, the reasoning goes," he said. Most of the murders happened in the regime's early years, when the situation was unstable.

For his part, friend and broadcast journalist Miguel Huerta said that those families who were not directly affected by the regime would understandably have a different perspective on the history than those who did have relatives murdered, killed or disappeared.

Pro-Pinochet sentiment from ordinary citizens

Pro-Pinochet sentiment is offered voluntarily and without hesitation from ordinary people on the street.

People like Señora Carmen.

She's a retired teacher who used to work in one of Santiago's poorest neighborhoods. We met at Santiago's Biblioplaza a little more than a week ago.

"Things were better during the dictatorship," she said, unprompted, when I asked her how her former students whom she taught for four consecutive years were doing. "There was more order then. More control. There was respect."

A woman working in a bakery in downtown Valparaíso offered nearly the identical words when I asked her how long she had been working there.

"Twenty three years," she answered.

"I imagine that Chile's changed a lot since then," I said.

"It has, and for the worse," the woman replied before launching into a praise of the tight control, order and lower levels of drugs that existed during the Pinochet regime.

Luis, a cab driver who took us from our apartment to the tony St. George's school on the city's outskirts, agreed.

He issued a passionate and unprompted denunciation of the dirt, sloth, drunkenness and general grime that permeated the city during Allende's

1,000 days in power. Pinochet cleaned things up, made the place more modern and got people to sleep at a more regular hour, declared the mustachioed driver, 67, who has been driving in Santiago for nearly half a century.

Alfredo Inostroza, a 64-year-old security guard at all-purpose store Falebella, said he remembers when Pinochet came to power as well as the years afterward.

"There was a fear," said Inostroza, a trim man with glasses and greying hair parted on the side that carries his seriousness and dignity. "The streets were much more empty." But Inostroza does not necessarily equate the fear with a negative assessment of the general´s leadership.

"Things were very unstable under Allende," he said. "The economy grew during Pinochet."

And Maria Eliana Eberhard, a prominent anesthetist, told us that her staunch anti-communism comes from the pain caused by her brother-in-law´s brother being killed by a communist. A shadow crossed over her normally exuberant face as she recounted the memory.

Personal ties in presidential campaign

Perhaps nowhere are the divided country and memories more visible than in the current presidential campaign, which, for the first time in the nation´s history, pits two women candidates against each other.

The first, of course, is Bachelet. The former president and a divorced mother of three children, she served as Defense Minister at the same time as Donald Rumsfeld held that position in the United States.

She is also the daughter of a former Chilean Air Force General.

So, too, is Evelyn Matthei, her opponent.

Ironically, their childhoods bore many similarities.

Both were daughters of Air Force generals who grew up in privilege, attending elite private schools and mastering several languages as well as a profession or skill that required extensive practice and training. (Bachelet is a certified pediatrician, while Matthei is a classically trained pianist.)

The two not only knew each other, but were childhood friends.

It was during the Pinochet era, though, that the similarities ended.

Whereas Matthei's father was part of the junta, Bachelet's father Alberto remained loyal to the constitution and to Allende. Because of that, he was tortured for months. Eventually he died at the Air Force Academy headed by the elder Matthei, who was not there at the time Bachelet's torture occurred.

Bachelet and her mother both were tortured as well in the infamous Villa Grimaldi compound where legions of others also were abused, murdered and disappeared.

Even though she did not break, Bachelet has said that she still grapples with the emotional scars from that experience.

Author Heraldo Muñoz has written about how Bachelet would see one of her torturers in the elevator of the building in which she lived.

One day, she confronted the man, telling him, "I know who you are. I have not forgotten."

The man averted his gaze during subsequent trips.

Bachelet has at different points shown compassion for the torturers, saying they carry bags of guilt with them. And when she was elected president, she offered a gesture of reconciliation to the elder Matthei, hugging him and calling him, "Uncle Fernando." (Her opponent has said her father and Bachelet's father were friends.)

In her initial comments after being chosen by her party following Pablo Longueira's surprise withdrawal from the race, Matthei asserted that Bachelet was eminently beatable.

That remains to be seen.

So, too, does the question of whether the election of either woman will inch this beautiful, blood-soaked land further away from its wounded past and closer to a more shared and united present.

The Week of Memory Begins

Posted on September 3, 2013

Ricardo Brodsky, director of the Museum of Memory and Human Rights.
(Photo courtesy of Jeff Kelly Lowenstein)

Something extraordinary is happening in Chile this week.

All across the country, from Arica to Punta Arenas, and in 30 of the 32 comunas, or districts, within Santiago, public discussion is happening about the coup on September 11, 1973 that was headed by Gen. Augusto Pinochet that ousted democratically-elected President Salvador Allende and ushered in 17 years of military rule.

Tonight marked the beginning of the nation's first Week of Memory. Occurring against the backdrop of the November presidential election, the next seven days will feature previously hidden or unknown testimony, pictures, films and texts.

Four key notions of memory underpin the programs.

The first is memory as an antidote to future such tyranny and oppression happening again in the country—a thought that's captured in the statement that was said and projected on the screen in the front of the room, "Nunca más."

Never again.

The second conception of memory is a spur to greater levels of fulfillment of democratic principles, of the appreciation both of democracy's fragility and of the importance of working ceaselessly to protect and advance its flow.

The third notion, according to Ricardo Brodsky, the director of the national Museum of Human Rights and Memory, is of memory as a restorative and reparative act that confers dignity that was previously stripped and violated to the victims.

And the fourth is the idea that the lessons of history and the suffering of the past must be taught to the next generation.

In his opening comments at a kickoff event at the Providencia Public Library, Brodsky noted that this is not the first time that a round number of the coup's anniversary has been commemorated.

However, as opposed to 20 years ago, when it was marked by a state ceremony, this year the conversations are happening in civil forums, in places like universities and conference halls and libraries.

The latter is where Dunreith and I went to the kickoff event. Originally slated to take place outside under a white tent set up next to the branch of the public library that sits in Parque Bustamante, the gathering was moved inside to the basement because of a light drizzle. The room was largely filled to capacity by close to 100 people of various ages who sat in stiff red chairs.

Recently elected Providencia Mayor Josefa Errázuriz talked about the comuna's decision, taken after fierce debate, to reverse the name that had been given to one of Providencia's major streets in 1980 as Ave. 11 September to its original name of New Providencia Avenue. She led the fight, she said, because she didn't want young people to receive any shred of a message that the date was one to be honored. It's inconceivable that homage would be given to that name, Errázuriz said.

She added that the street's renaming was a significant step in an ongoing process of helping to convert the sorrow, hurt and anger from the coup and the Pinochet years and dictatorship into future projects and plans.

"We need to put the new generation in touch with how we lived and suffered," she said. "The pain has to give place to proposals for the future."

We have to do it, she told me later, during a short break in which various types of cheese garnished with nuts and fruit juices, soft drinks and wine were all available.

The program's feature event was a showing of the 1978 German documentary film *Los Muertos No Callan*, or *The Dead Are Not Silent*. The crowd watched with a fierce and silent attention that was broken occasionally by a sigh or gasp.

Filmed in grainy black and white images, the movie told the story of the assassinations of top Allende political figures like Vice President Carlos Prats, Defense Secretary José Tohá and Ambassador to the United States Orlando Letelier.

But if the murdered politicians were silent, their widows gave voice to what happened. In the movie Moy de Tohá and Isabel Letelier narrate their horrific experience with almost unthinkable calm and composure and remarkable detail, even as their faces bear the toll that their husbands' murders and the recounting of their deaths takes on them.

The deaths happened after forces loyal to Pinochet, who had repeatedly declared his loyalty to Allende, bombed La Moneda, the President's palace. Fire and plumes of smoke billow on the screen for what feels like agonizing minutes, each successive flame further destroying the democratic ideals on which the nation had been based for nearly half a century.

The coup marked the beginning of Pinochet's ruthless reign in which Tohá, Letelier and many other leaders who were loyal to Allende were imprisoned at Isla Dawson, an island about 100 kilometers south of Punta Arenas. Tohá's death came after months of torture—the Pinochet government told the family that he had committed suicide—and after his wife had confronted the dictator.

"I am not talking to the head of the military junta," said Moy de Tohá. "I am talking to the man who we hosted at our house many times." Pinochet had done more than visit.

One of the film's most biting segments comes when his words of effusive praise for the Tohás, which he wrote by hand in a letter and had engraved on a plate, are shown repeatedly on the screen. Moy de Tohá also shows a card signed by 39 of her husband's fellow inmates who had also been incarcerated on Isla Dawson. Orlando Letelier was among the signatories.

Letelier moved to Washington after political pressure led to his release from prison and his eventual reunion with his family in Venzuela. He became one of the major voices of the Chilean resistance. On Sept. 10, 1976, he was deprived of his Chilean citizenship. During a solidarity concert that evening that was headlined by Joan Baez, he declared, "I was born Chilean, I am Chilean and I will die Chilean." Letelier then took square aim at the dictator.

"Pinochet was born a traitor and fascist. He is a traitor and fascist. He will die as a traitor and fascist," Letelier said.

Chilean secret police agents assassinated Letelier in a car bombing 11 days later. The bomb also claimed the life of his assistant Ronni Moffitt.

The Dead Are Not Silent ends after Isabel Letelier describes her fight to get to see her murdered husband. His eyes were still open. In his eyes, she said, she saw all of the regime's horror. But she also saw the strength necessary to carry on and continue fighting.

Isabel Letelier was in the front row of the audience at our screening. She walked unsteadily, the product of having recently lost the use of one of her eyes. But her diminished physical state did not mean that her contribution went unrecognized.

Quite the opposite, in fact.

During his comments in the panel after the film, Juan Guzmán, the former right-wing judge who indicted Pinochet shortly before his death, paid tribute to the courage, valor and strength of both widows. The crowd applauded for a long time, and again as Isabel Letelier left the room shortly before the panel ended.

I asked Guzmán about the people who had chanted, "They never got him" after Pinochet's death, referring to the fact that the former dictator eluded prison time during his lifetime. Guzmán had said these people hadn't learned anything as of the time of Pinochet's passing.

"Had these people still not learned the lessons of history," I asked?

"Many of them had not," he said.

Providencia councilman Jaime Parada, who is openly gay, addressed the same issue in response to a question I asked about why so many people we had met asserted that life was better under Pinochet.

"I come from a right wing family, and I remember my mother and father crying when Pinochet lost the plebiscite vote," he said. "Forty three percent of the country supported Pinochet during that vote—and many of them still do," he said.

This happened because of a confluence of factors, according to Parada. He cited the neo-liberal ideology that encouraged people to think only about themselves, and not to concern themselves with the pain of others. Parada also said that the country was in an extreme anti-Marxist position during the Cold War. At the same time, he also made the point that human rights violations abuse did not only occur during the dictatorship, but continue today in Chile and nations throughout the world.

"These abuses occur to women, to people with disabilities, and to gay, lesbian and transsexual people, among others," Parada said.

The unfinished work that memory calls us to do hung in the room as the session wrapped up at 10:00 p.m. and the group started to disperse into the warm evening. Practically bursting with all that we had seen and heard, Dunreith and I walked back to our apartment faster than usual.

The conversations about Chile's past would continue throughout the country the next day.

The Incomplete Victory of Villa Grimaldi

Posted on September 9, 2013

A sketch of a prisoner comforting another prisoner
who has been tortured at Villa Grimaldi.
(Photo courtesy of Jeff Kelly Lowenstein)

Of all the many disturbing details at Villa Grimaldi, the former restaurant turned torture center turned peace park, perhaps the most unnerving was learning about the sounds of children playing at a pool.

By itself, of course, the noises of children joyfully splashing around in water with their parents need not be a cause for distress. But Villa Grimaldi during the Pinochet years was no normal place.

The people hearing the children's pleasure were prisoners being held, blindfolded and beaten, in a red tower just yards away from the pool. A tower where prisoners were tortured at Villa Grimaldi.

Some of the parents were those who had tortured the prisoners, who were men and women, opponents real and imagined, old and young. They made their victims stand in excruciating positions, shocked them with devastating volts of electricity, violated them in nearly every way imaginable. Then, off-duty, they took their children with them to relax and enjoy a weekend afternoon.

In *Hitler's Willing Executioners*, Daniel Jonah Goldhagen wrote about the festive atmosphere and energy many Nazis brought to their assigned tasks of murdering Jews during the Holocaust.

We've also learned about the families of high-ranking Nazis who lived near death camps and developed a sense of normalcy and routine.

South Africa's Truth and Reconciliation Commission and Rian Malan's book *My Traitor's Heart* revealed tales of apartheid-era guards killing a black South African and having a barbecue while the man's flesh burned nearby.

But never before have I heard about this integration, this immersion, this utter lack of self-consciousness that all standards of decency and self-respect have been eroded.

I am not suggesting that there was virtue in the other examples of barbarity, but rather that for me this marked a new low.

It is important to note that we do not know that this happened because the DINA guards told us that it occurred. They and those responsible for the place destroyed everything that they could, as oppressors and torturers and abusers often do, committing not only the first crime of violation, but attempting the second crime of denial. Rather we know that these things happened because they were constructed from the memories of the survivors.

So, too, was the small wooden shack built on the other side of the villa. Inside the shack are black and white sketches drawn by former detainees. One shows an inmate leaning down to comfort another who is prostrate on the ground after having been tortured. A sketch of a prisoner comforting another prisoner who has been tortured at Villa Grimaldi.

In this way, and in many others, Villa Grimaldi represents the triumph of memory over forgetting.

Set in a residential neighborhood in the neighborhood of La Reina, the compound, like its country, appears hermetically sealed from the world. Passing through the red brick gate, one enters a green space whose air is filled with the cacophony of light green birds that look like parrots. The reminders of the place's bloody past are everywhere.

They're in the gallery of black and white photographs that a pair of women with red shirts were studying solemnly.

The sentence, "No podemos ni queremos olvidar," stands in large black letters underneath the images.

We cannot nor do we want to forget.

They're in an enormous metal cube that stands on one of its corners. Opening the door and entering the dark interior, one sees the rusted pieces of railway tracks that were used to weigh down the bodies of murdered victims before they were thrown from helicopters by Pinochet's minions into the ocean. The tactic worked for the disposal of many, but not all, of the victims.

Such as the body of Marta Ugarte, a revolutionary opponent of the dictatorship, which washed up in 1976. The Chilean newspaper of record, *El Mercurio*, reported her death as a love affair gone wrong, but a crack had appeared in the facade of the wall of silence Pinochet had erected.

A picture of Ugarte, along with a handwritten letter, appears in one of the few rooms that still stood after the facility was destroyed. The room also contains photographs and articles and personal items of many others of the thousands killed during the murderous regime.

The names of the people killed are listed on a memorial wall in chronological order in a corner of the park.

The oppression went in phases, with the regime focused at different times on the communists, the MIRistas, or violent revolutionaries, and labor organizers. The early years of the regime, 1974 to 1976, saw the highest level of killing.

The peace park, which opened in 1997, has a rose garden dedicated to the women who were tortured and killed there. Small mosaic plaques that each have a rose placed on their side dot the park. Political parties like the communists have also created memorials for those who suffered the same fate.

A rose garden that honors women victims at Villa Grimaldi.
(Photo courtesy of Jeff Kelly Lowenstein)

The door through which prisoners used to be brought is locked.

On the ground near the door is another plaque which states the door's former purpose and declares that it will never be opened again. A mosaic-covered stone in the shape of many leaves extends from the door instead.

Each of the elements in the park—aspects that include an international conference preceded by an adaptation of Euripides' *The Supplicants* and a poem by Oscar Hahn that concludes with the line, "The bone is a hero of resistance"—embody Chile's effort to honor the victims and remember that deadly era in its history so that it never happens again.

Indeed, each name, each age recorded, each painstaking detail noted also represents a small victory for memory over oblivion.

Yet they are also incomplete. This is so for several reasons.

The first and most basic is that, as Martha Minow wrote in the introduction to her book, *Between Vengeance and Forgiveness*, any attempt at memory after coming together after mass violence is both necessary yet inevitably insufficient because it cannot undo the trauma that has already occurred.

The second is that, as Patricio Guzmán shows us in the film *Nostalgia for the Light*, the record is incomplete.

There are still women combing the Atacama Desert and looking in the Andes Mountains for the remains of their loved ones. There are still the disappeared who have not reappeared, whose precise fates are not known. Beyond that, there are many in Chile who do not want to allow themselves to know about their country's past.

Dunreith and I asked the guard at Plaza Egaña, the Metro station a couple of miles away from the compound, how to get to Villa Grimaldi.

He said he didn't know.

Neither did the woman who sold tickets at the station.

Or our taxi driver, a young man with a beard and ponytail, who drove us up and down the street on which Villa Grimaldi is located.

Barbara Azcárraga, a guide at the villa and a Master's student in history who is doing memory-related projects at Catholic University and the Museum of Memory and Human Rights, said many Chileans do not know about the Villa.

"The subject is taboo," she said.

She also explained that many policemen live a few blocks away from the villa and don't like its presence or mission. The retired military people who live near the policemen feel the same way.

And yet Manuel Contreras, the former DINA head who oversaw its brutal operations, is incarcerated nearby.

Chile lives in this state of incomplete victory. Half the country said in a national poll that they want to turn the page on the nation's past, yet on a different question 80 percent said they want their children to learn about the past.

As Hugo Rojas and others have noted, serious questions remain about what the third generation will learn about the 1973 coup a half-century after it occurred.

But what is clear from going to Villa Grimaldi is that there is a cadre of people in the country who have committed themselves to confronting what happened there, to documenting it and honoring those who were abused and killed, and to striving with all that they have to ensure that such torture does not happen again in this once and now-again peaceful nation.

Memory Ceremony with Michelle Bachelet at Villa Grimaldi

Posted on September 10, 2013

The fortieth anniversary of the Pinochet coup that removed democratically-elected leader Salvador Allende from power has been met with a blizzard of activity.

Dunreith and I have attended many, but far from all, of the events. Documentary films. Academic conferences. A translated version of Euripides' play *The Supplicants*. Round table discussions on the importance of memory.

Nothing moved us like seeing the relatives of the disappeared today at Villa Grimaldi, the former restaurant turned torture center turned peace park.

I was part of a pack of about 50 photographers, videographers and radio reporters that took pictures from every possible angle of Michelle Bachelet, the former president and current presidential front runner who, along with her mother Ángela Jeria, was detained and tortured during the military dictatorship.

But what got me the deepest was meeting people like Cecilia Hernandez, who was wearing a picture of her mustachioed brother Juan pinned to her purple jacket.

Cecilia was 13 years old when the coup happened. She remembers the terror she felt. She remembers being threatened, with her three-year-old sister, by the authorities, who along with their dignity and sense of safety robbed their home of many of its most valuable items.

They also took Juan, her older brother.

Two years after the coup, in 1975, Juan, who was politically active against the regime, left for Mendoza, Argentina. The authorities went there, brought him back, and detained him in Villa Grimaldi. In June 1976 Juan was disappeared.

He hasn't returned to this day, Cecilia said, a cloud of sadness and grief hanging over her face.

She was one of hundreds of people who sat in the white chairs underneath a large outdoor tent. Every other chair had a black and white picture of someone who had been murdered at Villa Grimaldi. Each photograph had the person's name underneath and a red rose laid across the chair. At the event, organized by a coalition of human rights groups, the families stood and raised the pictures during a song that paid tribute to their loved ones.

Through their comments, event organizers made it clear that the day was not just about honoring and remembering the dead, but about demanding complete truth and full justice.

Lorena Pizarro has been president of the Group of Families of Detained and Disappeared People since 2003. She issued a fiery speech, but she also made the point that for her the day was one of happiness.

"The loved ones have not been forgotten," said Pizarro, whose father was disappeared. "They have been with us every day of the past 40 years."

They were there in the full-throated call issued by a woman near the front of the tent after singer Isabel Aldunate finished her final song.

"Compañeras, detained and disappeared?" the woman yelled before the applause for the song had stopped.

"Presente," the crowd answered as one.

Present.

"Compañeros, detained and disappeared?" She asked, louder and slower, lingering over every syllable.

"Presente."

Louder. More united.

"Compañeras, executed for political reasons?"

"Presente."

"Compañeros, executed for political reasons?"

"Presente."

Louder still.

The call and response concluded with a salute to Salvador Allende's ideals, now and forever, before family members placed the pictures and the roses at the wall that honors Villa Grimaldi's victims.

Dunreith and I started to move away from the pack that continued to follow every inch of Bachelet's slow walk out of the compound. We walked past Jeria, who had linked her arm with a young man wearing a dark suit and, unlike her daughter, was attracting no attention. We crossed the street, caught a bus and rode quietly to the Metro station on our way back to Diego Portales University.

The swelling in my heart and the lump in my throat remained.

A Day of Memory in Three Parts

Posted on September 11, 2013

A shattered half spectacle at the Museum of Memory and Human Rights.
(Photo courtesy of Jeff Kelly Lowenstein)

Part I: Parroquia la Anunciación

A humble room with red brick and a largely bare white wall.

A large wooden cross with a chip on one side and a portrait of a bearded Jesus beneath it.

A warm feeling of reunion filling the cold air and dark room, of people hugging each other hard and long.

Percival Cowley, a pastor radiating with the goodness that comes from having been part of the tradition of church leaders who fight for justice, of Niemoller and Romero and Tutu and Lapsley. A man who donned a white scarf with red crosses and who spoke, in an even, deep voice about remembering the coup that took place 40 years ago today.

A man who also spoke about the ordinary violence and abuse that continues today, the failures to give poor people their just dignity and respect, and the economic, moral and social violence that endures and that keeps Chile from being a just country.

Josefa Errázuriz, the newly elected mayor of Providencia, the section of Santiago where we live. A woman with short brown hair and fierce determination who defeated the incumbent, a man who used to work for Pinochet's secret police and said his qualifications were that he was an effective project manager.

A leader who included many sectors of the community in the ceremony of memory and welcomed all types of people into the room.

A group of three Communists who stood on one side of the room holding a flag that honored a slain comrade.

The old.

The young.

The women.

And the Mapuche, the indigenous people who came forward in their traditional dress and spoke in Mapudungun, their language, and in Spanish, expressing their gratitude for being included in the ceremony and the community.

The kiss on the cheek between Maria Jesus Aleñir, one of the Mapuche women, and Cowley.

The resolve in the room that the atrocities of the past should never happen again.

After the ceremony ended, Cowley told me about having heard about the coup the night before it happened and walking the streets in the early morning of September 11 40 years ago.

Silence.

Realizing the next day that everything was changing.

Having to stay inside for three days. Then, when he and so many others, were allowed to go out, seeing the brutality of the regime instantly being visited on people in the southern part of Santiago.

"We thought the military was different from other soldiers in Latin America," he said. "We were right. They were more brutal."

The words of Emilio, a young Communist whose mother fled the country to Holland and whose grandfather was detained and tortured, along with so many others, in the National Stadium.

It's important for us to learn about the past, he said, because we need to know about this era of comprehensive unconstitutionality.

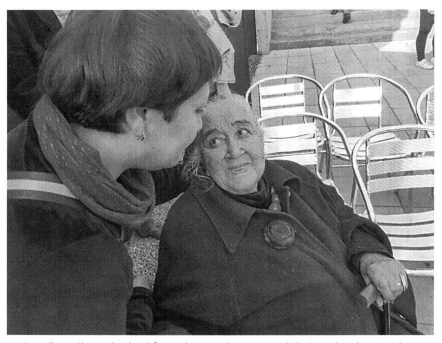

Ana González, who had five relatives disappeared during the dictatorship, at the Museum of Memory and Human Rights.
(Photo courtesy of Jeff Kelly Lowenstein)

Part II: Museum of Memory and Human Rights

The giant shattered half spectacle of Salvador Allende greeting you as you walk down the smooth surface toward the open amphitheater.

A circle of chairs arranged in pairs.

An actor dressed as Allende, with his beard and three-piece suit coated in parts with dust, walking stiffly to the middle of the circle, and starting to read in a calm, yet emotion-filled voice on the people's radio station his final address to the nation.

"I will not resign," he says before going on to thank all the groups of people who had put their trust in him as a servant of the Constitution.

"I will pay for loyalty to the people with my life," he says.

"Viva Chile!" he declares at the end of his speech.

"Viva Chile!" The group of people, actors themselves, answer, standing outside the circle in a line traced by roses placed and ashes on the ground, holding white handkerchiefs aloft in the air. One of them had herself been tortured during the dictatorshiop.

"Viva Chile!" The people respond, including Ana González, a sturdy woman with long, lush red nails, a thick red necklace, a cane and a warm, open face and whose husband, two sons and pregnant daughter-in-law were all disappeared during the dictatorship.

"Viva Chile!" Señora Ana yelled, cupping her hands so that her voice would project farther.

Señora Ana, who sat because walking is difficult and who was treated as royalty by women and men who sought her out or wanted a hug or combed her long, grey hair.

Señora Ana, who wrote down her number and motioned for me to call her so that I would stop asking her questions and she could listen to the testimonies that were projected from the center of the circle to the open space.

The actors walking into the space after the man playing Allende walked out, sitting in the chairs and reading the testimonies they had been given to each other as a horde of photographers and videographers and radio reporters, myself included, crept ever closer.

A woman with the picture of a relative weeping and being comforted by another woman who enveloped her in her arms and did not let her go.

The large Chilean flag flanked by two black flags billowing in the gentle breeze in the mid-afternoon sun.

The rows of colorful pictures drawn by children of the disappeared titled *Aquí están*.

Here they are.

The answer to the question that primarily mothers and sisters and aunts and grandmothers of incalculable courage asked in Chile and Argentina, the neighboring countries where tens of thousands of people were disappeared, sometimes during the night, almost always never to be seen again.

The pictures that were drawn by children as young as three and as old as 17. But whichever age the children were the images were filled with love for, and connection to, the mother or father who had been taken from them.

A two-sided exhibit of photographs taken by Edward Shaw on the streets of Buenos Aires in the early 80s. Pictures of outlined bodies in subway stations and on advertisements with the family member's name, date of birth and, sometimes, a question mark.

Or the words, "Aparición con vida."

Appearing with life.

The crowd that swelled and grew and watched and listened and cried and talked and laughed.

The sounds of the testimony and the rapt attention of friend and memory scholar Hugo Rojas as he listened while we walked back up the smooth slope to the Metro Station.

Part III: Communist and Socialist Vigil at Estadio Nacional

Being deposited by the bus in front of the stadium that was transformed by the dictatorship into a torture chamber.

The memories of Grateful Dead concerts being sparked, with the combination of commerce and common conviction and passion for the cause and peaceful mingling and a decentralized yet unified feel.

A young boy sitting on his father's shoulders and carrying a large red flag.

Dozens and dozens of candles being lit.

Hand-written poems.

A row of shoes made of clear tape.

Pictures of Allende.

Calls for truth and justice.

The crowd gathering and growing as the sun made its way down and began to mark the end of the day.

The quiet on the city's streets as nearly all shops closed up early for the evening in anticipation of greater violence than there's been before.

The knowledge that Chile's wounds will still be there tomorrow, but having to think that today made a positive difference.

Gratitude to Dunreith for joining me on our journey.

Memory.

September 18 Celebrations Start in Providencia

Posted on September 13, 2013

Dancing the cueca at a pre-September 18 party near our apartment.
(Photo courtesy of Jeff Kelly Lowenstein)

Even though September 18 isn't for five more days, you don't have to work hard to find an Independence Day celebration here in Chile right now.

You just have to follow the music.

Dunreith and I had just returned from picking up our visa to go to Brazil in October when we heard the loud thumping music, full of accordions, pulsing from the ground up to our thirteenth floor balcony. Bound by journalistic duty, I told my beloved wife I would be back soon.

I took the elevator down to the first floor, walked right, walked left and then right again on Padre Mariano. The music drew me like a piece of metal to a magnet. Louder as I went one street north to La Concepción. More accordions and singing. I turned around the corner of a multi-story office building and saw the fence to the backyard slightly ajar. Inside were dozens of Chileans at varying levels of sobriety—"bebiendo, bailando, comiendo y disfrutando."

Drinking.

Dancing.

Eating.

Partying.

The smoke from the grill that was cooking rows of anticucho—barbequed meat on a skewer—hit me as I passed through the opening in the gate. Red, white and blue streamers, balloons and Chilean flags lined the walls. In the center were men and women in traditional dress and garb dancing with skill and abandon.

They finished one song. The crowd that formed in a ring around them applauded, then started chanting, "Cue-ca, cue-ca, cue-ca," for the national dance. The dancers obliged with a flurry of handkerchiefs, drawing men and women from the group to join them.

They consented gratefully.

Next to the dancing stretched the end of a line of people waiting their turn to try to throw three hoops around the necks of bottles of alcohol that stuck out from a bed of straw. One man won a bottle of red and white wine in his three throws. The other people in the line eyed him with admiration and a tinge of jealousy.

I was shooting pictures with abandon while trying to heed the words of a Chilean photographer at one of the September 11 events who had politely encouraged me to not block people's views, when one of the dancers approached.

"Where are you from?" asked a man with a kind face, who was probably in his 50s and wearing a black hat. I told him that I was from the United States.

"This is the first time I've been here in Chile for Dieciocho, for the 18th," I told him.

"Do you want to take a picture with us?" he wondered, motioning to the rest of the dancers.

"Of course," I replied, starting to walk toward the eight of them.

"No," my new friend said. "With your camera."

Right.

I gave him my Lumix with just a hint of trepidation—many people looked like they had not waited for noon to start celebrating—and he snapped a shot of me with the group.

We shook hands as the group dispersed for the moment.

A woman near the wall on the side of the parking lot waved to the woman who was working the grill. The grill lady smiled. A couple of minutes later, she thrust my first anticucho in my hand.

It's a national treat of skewered beef and sausage stuck firmly on top of each other. Salty and cooked right through. I could see my trajectory if I chose to stay, so started to walk back through the gate.

"Don't forget to have more anticucho and, of course, Terremotos," a disembodied voice urged the revelers.

Dunreith and I learned last week from the adult students in our English conversation class that a Terremoto is a deceptively potent drink that consists of white wine, pisco, ice cream and sugar.

"You have to try it," they told us.

I wasn't quite ready for the earth to rumble, so maintained my focus and kept walking home.

The sounds of the music grew fainter as I approached our apartment.

The Rodeo at Parque Alberto Hurtado

Posted on September 16, 2013

Two caballeros about to knock down a cow at Parque Alberto Hurtado.
(Photo courtesy of Jeff Kelly Lowenstein)

"What are you doing?" the photographer standing next to me in the sandy rodeo ring asked me in Spanish as I raised my Panasonic DMCZS25 to take a picture of the black and white, mangy-looking cow that had just been knocked to the ground by a pair of horsemen wearing sombreros and traditional cloaks.

I thought the answer was pretty obvious.

Trying to stay out of the way of the horses that were standing in a row and whose back legs seemed within kicking range, for one. At the same time, avoiding the other horses who were being ridden sideways by the cowboys in the middle of the sandy ring.

Nevertheless, I was aware both of being a guest in the country and, more to the point, of standing near the side of a small stadium with about three dozen horses on all sides of me.

Their riders were contestants at Parque Alberto Hurtado during Semana de la Chilenidad, a week of typical Chilean cultural activities that started before, and ended after, Chilean Independence Day on September 18. (It's often simply called, "Dieciocho.") Rodeo was named the national sport of Chile in 1962.

"I'm taking a picture," I answered.

"You can't take pictures of cows that have fallen," replied the photographer, who was about my height, stocky, and was wearing a woolen black hat and round glasses.

"It's forbidden," he told me.

He went on to explain that there were strict rules governing the photographing of cows in the rodeo competition. Violators, he said meaningfully, can be arrested by the carabineros, citing an example of one recent photographer who had been hit forcefully in the head after having taken a rules-breaking image.

I looked at the first row in the stand outside of the ring. The number of green-suited carabineros standing with arms folded right near the spot where I had gained entrance half an hour earlier seemed to have multiplied. Perhaps I was being unduly influenced by my new acquaintance, but some of them seemed to be looking at me.

I tried to see where I could leave the ring without being noticed. The fact that I had snapped two pictures of the same cow on the ground after it had been ploughed into the ring's sideboards gave my search additional urgency.

I pictured attempting to inform Dunreith, who, after a cursory glance at the cowboys coming into the stadium, listening to the white-robed priest bless the event, and hearing the Chilean and Spanish national anthems, had returned to the Adam Johnson novel she had been reading. (I had a sneaking suspicion that she would not notice me being carted off into custody.)

"Where are you from?" asked my new acquaintance, interrupting my reverie.

"I'm from the United States; it's my first time here in the country for Dieciocho," I replied. Because he had conveyed the information to me about my transgression, I started talking to the photographer as if he were a policeman.

"Thank you for explaining rules I wasn't aware of," I said, a touch of desperation entering my voice as I imagined myself standing before a Chilean judge and hoping that ignorance of rodeo photography policy would in fact be an acceptable excuse.

"Is there anything else that I shouldn't do?" I asked.

"Don't take pictures of a cow that's on the ground," he repeated.

I decided to change the topic.

"Is this a national competition?" I inquired.

My question elicited a lengthy discourse about the association of local rodeos, the winners of whom earned points that helped qualify them for the annual national competition in April. The man spoke calmly, as if we were having an afternoon cup of tea, and not standing within striking range of large hoofed animals who could easily paralyze, maim or even kill us with a single kick of their back legs.

"What's your name?" he asked.

I told him mine and requested the same information.

"Maximiliano," he answered, smiling broadly and extending his hand.

I shook it. His calloused hand had a firm grip. We started talking about where we worked.

Maximiliano was independent, he said. This meant freelance.

I started telling him about the Fulbright and teaching a journalism class at Diego Portales University.

Maximiliano nodded sagely, then asked, "Where's your credential?"

Uh-oh.

"I didn't have one," I said, that sinking feeling again coursing through my stomach. " I asked the man at the gate if it was all right if I went in, and he let me."

To be completely honest, the second part of the statement was far more accurate than the first. (Unless you count a look at the gatekeeper who pulled it open and allowed me to slip through as asking.)

I looked again in the stands.

More carabineros.

Another cow being crushed into the board near me.

The time when I had entered the stadium in the park and walked along green grass, past the little children being led on ponies by a blue-haired lady and close to a dozen people playing on the longest fussball table I had ever seen, seemed like years ago.

I scanned the crowd to find Dunreith. Her attention was directed downward into the book. It was time for me to leave, but how?

I spied a cowboy directing a horse toward the same exit where I had entered. This was my chance. I gave enough space to avoid the row of horses waiting their turn as well as the one shimmying around the middle of the ring and arrived at the open gate just a second after the horse.

True to his name, the caballero let me pass. I walked up the bald patch of dirt, nearly bumping into four carabineros. They paid no attention to me.

I walked back into the stands and found Dunreith, who looked quizzically at me.

"I didn't see you, so I started to walk around," she told me.

We confirmed that we were both ready to leave and started to head back toward the entrance of the park. Before we left the stadium I shook a security guard's hand and thanked him.

"Where are you from?" he asked.

"The United States," I said.

"Which state?"

"From Chicago in the state of Illinois. It's our first time in the country, our first Dieciocho. We're very excited to be here. "

This was starting to sound too much like my conversation with Maximiliano. Better not to push my luck.

"Thanks again," I repeated, reaching my hand out again. Disappointment flashed across the guard's dark face for an instant before he extended his hand and we shook again.

We stopped to buy an overpriced cheese empanada with a flaky crust and my second anticucho, a long skewer with a cork on the bottom, thick hunks of meat, slices of thin red peppers and onion in between, and a piece of bread on the top. Unlike much Chilean asado that I'd had thus far, which has been on the overcooked side, this anticucho had a savory medium rare texture.

My gratitude at being free after my excursion into the ring made it taste even better.

Meeting Patricio and Andrés at Estadio Nacional

Posted on September 17, 2013

Andrés and Patricio at the fondo at the National Stadium.
(Photo courtesy of Jeff Kelly Lowenstein)

Part I: Selling T-Shirts at Fenway, the Sausage King

I sold Green Monster and Bleacher Creature t-shirts at Fenway Park during the summer of 1990.

The season was noteworthy for a number of reasons.

I became firm friends with fellow vendor David Axelrad—a connection that has continued until today.

Since we were selling right outside Gate E on Lansdowne Street, I had one of the best possible spots near Fenway Park. Yet, as meaningful as these all ultimately proved to be, one aspect stands above all:

We sold next to the Sausage King.

Gatesy and Jimmy, brothers and a pair of Italian-Irish Boston Police officers, owned and ran the stand as a second job. Tickets scalpers and policemen would gather at the King for a brief chat in what amounted to the equivalent of the demilitarized zone established between the Koreas.

In addition to the sausages that had hefty portions of Windex that dribbled down from a glass window onto the grill, the stand was distinctive because of Perry's hawking.

A welterweight boxer who hailed from South Boston, Perry would spend large chunks of time admiring his tanned biceps and issuing calls to attract customers like "How many, how many, my name is Jack Benny," and "Coast to coast, like buttered toast, we sell the most."

Perry often punctuated his favorite jingles with a guttural sound, "AAAAHHHH!"

His relentless desire to scam the customer knew no limits. When Mike, a pretzel salesman who would have far preferred to practice astrology, left his stand for a minute, Perry stepped in, charged the unsuspecting client two dollars instead of one and then pocketed the change.

His favorite story was how he took a $100 bill from a drunken customer in a limousine who thought he had give him $10. Perry returned $2 to the man and declared solemnly, "We're even."

Memories of Perry's antics stirred within me late this afternoon when I met Patricio and Andrés at one of the many anticucho stands outside the National Stadium that is the site of the 14th annual Festival of Ñuñoa.

Part II: Festival De Ñuñoa

These fondos are happening in communities throughout Santiago in observance of "El Dieciocho," or Chilean Independence Day on September 18. Of course, the celebrations are by no means limited to that day only. In fact, one of the vendors at today's Dieciocho event told me that the hours of 10:00 a.m. to 1:00 a.m. from Tuesday through Sunday are actually light compared with the fondo at Bernardo O'Higgins that, like New York, never sleeps.

I met Andrés and Patricio on my second late afternoon lap around the stadium. I had already passed by vendors baking empanadas on the grill, the crust carrying bits of charcoal. I had observed a fussball game that involved three generations of family members and chatted with the owner of a shop that sold stuffed cupcakes with a replica of the Chilean flag made of frosting. I had seen a traditional Mapuche hut made of straw that stood next to a stand where a young woman with blue jeans who did not want to be photographed kneaded the dough that would turn into sopaipillas.

The blue sky had few clouds, the air was gently cool and couples old and young, groups of friends, and families strolled leisurely around the stadium, their pleasure in the national celebration and being with each other evident in their smiles and relaxed faces. Children who did not want to get off the rides they were on in the mini-amusement park near the front of the stadium wailed in protest.

The smoke billowing forth from the grill he was working and the sunglasses and bright red hat he was wearing obscured a view of Patricio's face until I walked to the other side of him. A construction worker, he is solidly built, has brown hair and moves with a decisive efficiency.

I took a picture first of Patricio, then of Andrés, who is stockier, younger and has a buzz cut that looks like it's been growing back for about a month.

They asked where the picture was going. I answered, and we started chatting.

Andrés' extolling the quality of the beef they were grilling in an effort to cajole customers whose ages ranged from teenager to senior citizens rivaled some of Perry's top efforts to help us sell t-shirts before demanding a commission after a successful sale. ("One hundred percent Egyptian cotton," he would crow, paying no attention to the fact that our cotton came from nowhere near Egypt.)

Andrés repeatedly asked me if I wanted a Terremoto, a trademark Chilean drink that Dunreith and I had agreed we would try tomorrow. My refusal neither deterred nor offended him. Instead he kept emphasizing the importance of our trying the alcoholic trifecta of a Terremoto, La Replica and a Tsunami. It sounded like a recipe for public drunkenness and free pickings for the many pickpockets we had been advised liked to feast on foreign prey at the fondos.

Andrés shows the pure quality of the beef he is about to cook.
(Photo courtesy of Jeff Kelly Lowenstein)

Part III: Patricio works the grill and an angle

For his part, Patricio called me over behind the red shack that was part of "La Pica Del Tio Nino," the spot where he was working that had been set up for the festival.

"I want you to get me a beer," he said.

"That's fine," I replied. "Just give me the money and I'll bring it over."

My answer did not appear to satisfy Patricio, who then said he wanted two beers. He then showed me a blue lined receipt with the words, "1 Anticucho" on it. All became clear.

I would purchase two beers, which were 1,000 peso each, and then bring them to Patricio and Andrés, who would in turn give me an anticucho from the receipt Patricio was about to hand me.

I would save 500 pesos off the price of the anticucho.

Patricio and Andrés would have the beer they coveted.

And the store would have 2,000 pesos it had not had before.

The plan went seamlessly.

Patricio hustled me over to the side of the shack, where he placed the beers with such care and reverence it was like he was putting a Faberge egg in its case. He offered me a cold coke he had already hidden, but my journalistic ethics against accepting gifts from sources compelled me to decline. Of course, these same ethics hadn't rebelled against my scamming the company they were working for not one minute earlier.

Somehow that seemed different.

I identified the anticucho I wanted, which, as Andrés pointed out to all who passed by, had 250 grams, or more than half a pound of fresh beef and sausage from Chillán, a community about four hours south of Santiago. We made sure the meat was cooked enough and I retreated to one of the Tio Nono tables that were covered with red and white tablecloths.

I had a long wooden skewer, two pieces each of beef and sausage and no plate.

No problem.

A woman instantly appeared not with a plate, but a plastic cup full of napkins. I needed all of them, as both the sausage and especially the beef were dripping with juice. The woman, who was dressed in an all-white outfit, recognized my plight and brought over even more napkins before I finished to help me clean my hands.

I thanked her, then returned to the grill.

In between his salting the meat, I learned that Andrés is 29 years old, works in concert promotion and has a wife and nine-year-old son.

Patricio has three children ranging from ages 15 to 24 and offered repeatedly to give Dunreith and me a tour of Santiago's most beautiful places. (We didn't talk about which those were.)

He leaned in to tell me that since I hadn't handed them the ticket for the anticucho, I could get another one later.

Pure Perry.

I responded in kind.

"I'll get two more Coronas and give them to you," I told Patricio. He smiled broadly.

"I don't forget," I said.

We all swapped phone numbers. I shook hands again with Patricio. Andrés and I hugged. I said I would come back with my wife the next day. My rumpled anticucho ticket in my pocket, I believed it at that moment.

I don't know if we'll make it back, but I do know that I appreciated the chance to meet Patricio and Andrés.

And to visit with Perry for a minute, too.

Terremoto 1, Jeff 0

Posted on September 18, 2013

I had done all the preparations.

Enjoyed the Journalism Department's celebration last Thursday.

Walked into a work party for "El Dieciocho,", Chile's Independence Day, last Friday.

Traveled by metro, bus and car to Alejandra Matus and Alberto Barrera's idllyic home nestled in the foothills of the mountains on Saturday.

Taken pictures of teams of caballeros herding cows into the wall at the rodeo at Parque Alberto Hurtado on Monday.

Evoked memories of Fenway Park circa 1990 by spending time with anticucho cooks and hustlers Patricio and Andrés at the National Stadium on Tuesday.

Today was the day. Dieciocho. And I was ready for the New York City of fondas, Parque Bernardo O'Higgins.

Or so I thought.

Patricio had told me yesterday that whereas the party at Estadio Nacional ended at 1:00 a.m., resuming at 10:00 the next morning, the fiesta at Parque O'Higgins never stops. It's also the site of La Jein Fonda, a venue for musical acts and performances.

Dunreith and I walked down the usually bustling Providencia Avenue to meet fellow Fulbrighter Larry Geri outside the Salvador Metro station. With very few exceptions, shops with steel gates announcing their closure greeted us.

Before leaving our apartment, we had heeded Alejandra's instructions, delivered via email, to empty our wallets of all non-essential items that we might fear losing. I didn't bring my customary fire-red backpack or my notebook. But I did have a to-do list.

At the very top: tasting my first Terremoto.

Multiple sources had advised me to try the drink. Juan, one of the doormen in the front lobby of our apartment, had thought seriously a week ago when I asked him what I should do during the week of Dieciocho.

"A Terremoto," he said after extensive deliberation.

He had repeated his recommendation last night when I observed that it was quite cold in the front lobby, as if the sweet drink with white wine, ice cream and cognac could magically ward off freezing weather.

In our session last Thursday the students in our English conversation class had also told us earnestly that we needed to try one of the drinks during Fiestas Patrias, the weeklong celebration that included today's commemoration of Independence Day.

We took the Metro to Los Heroes and managed to identify that the Parque O'Higgins stop was the correct one for us. We walked through the large gates, down the row of stands selling every conceivable kind of trinket, past the picture of "Hanoi Jane" that was drawn across the white tent that served as the venue for the musical entertainment, and into the sandy area where food was sold.

The smell of sizzling chicken, beef, veal and sausage being grilled on fresh charcoal assaulted me. A stand from Arica, one of Chile's northernmost communities, had a row of particularly juicy-looking chicken that caught my attention. I made a mental note to return after completing our quest.

Then I saw them.

Already prepared, the frothy white cream approaching the lip of the plastic cups that held them, six Terremotos in three different flavors stood atop a wooden bar. After determining that Dunreith was not going to have one, I invited Larry to join me.

He did.

I approached the woman behind the bar and delivered what had become my standard speech about how this is the first Dieciocho we had attended, that this was the first Terremoto we were drinking and thus this was an important moment in which we needed to have success.

She listened patiently, then directed me to the caja, the place where nearly all Chilean purchases occur, the spot where you pay and receive a paper receipt that you pass to the server.

I went through the same speech with the man at the caja. He listened with slightly less patience than the server, and said in a less than enthusiastic tone that he hoped I enjoyed myself.

I've found that at times explaining to people our purpose and the meaning of that particular moment in their country can elicit higher levels of service. This time nothing of the sort occurred.

But Larry and I did receive our desired drinks. He chose grenadine, while I picked mint. We toasted and took our first sips. The sweetness of the frothy substance at the top was cut by a beer-like taste in the body of the drink.

Dunreith pointed out that I was drinking on an empty stomach, so, after completing a lap around the food, entertainment and child amusement park options, we returned to the spot with the tasty-looking chicken breasts.

I tried to purchase the chicken directly from the woman working the grill, only to be told that I needed to go yet again to the caja. So I went inside the tent with signage that proclaimed its loyalty to Arica, located the caja and sought to take my chicken to go.

The lady at this caja told me that there was no takeaway option, that the chicken came with a salad and thus we had to sit down and wait for it. This was just fine with Larry, who recently lost the heat in his apartment, so was happy to soak in the early afternoon sun.

The waiting turned out to be longer than we had expected. Larry and I contented ourselves with making our way through the Terremoto, which was having no apparent effect on us.

A waiter with long black hair approached our table and asked us in English where we were from. I kept answering in Spanish, and put special emphasis on our desire to have our chicken as soon as possible. About a minute later, he walked through the tent carrying the chicken breast on the end of a long, thin, shiny fork. The meat and the salad of green tomatoes in a salty sauce arrived shortly after that.

As opposed to much grilled meat we'd encountered thus far, which was often cooked to the point of resembling jerky, if not leather, this breast was piping hot, tender and succulent. The conversation flowed amiably between us.

We talked about our kids, our teaching and research projects, his wife's impending visit and their plans to dance the tango in Buenos Aires. (She's been taking private lessons for months. He hasn't.)

We finished the chicken and decided we were ready to leave. The crowds were streaming into the park. Although the sidewalks were not yet jam-packed with people, we could tell that time was not far off.

"That Terremoto is starting to kick in," Larry said as we neared the front gate.

Indeed it was.

My stomach and head were starting to get the same woozy feeling I remembered having with some frequency during my freshman year at Stanford. My steps became more uneven, my pictures more erratic. I weaved through the ceaseless wave of people entering the park and staggered onto the Metro that would take us back to our apartment. Larry graciously allowed me to take a seat.

We parted at Salvador and made plans to eat dinner together with his wife and him next Monday. Dunreith, who was battling an upset stomach, and I walked the two blocks from Pedro de Valdivia in an unsteady gait.

The doormen greeted us.

Dunreith explained in Spanish that she had had enough of fondas. I said that I didn't feel that good and that the Terremoto had won.

They laughed. Loudly.

We made it into our apartment and took an hour-long nap to recover from our wild adventure.

We woke up at 5:10 p.m.

The sun was shining brightly.

The Terremoto was still rumbling away within me.

Patricio Guzmán's
Nostalgia for the Light

Posted on August 18, 2013

As a child in Chile, Patricio Guzmán stared at the stars and reveled in the untroubled quiet of a peaceful country, childhood and world.

Chile, as he explains in the introduction to his intricate, thought-provoking and haunting documentary film, *Nostalgia for the Light*, was disconnected from the rest of the world.

The presidents walked the streets unprotected.

But the country began to become integrated with the world as the Atacama Desert, a 600-mile stretch of land that is commonly considered to be the driest place in the world, became the site of some of the largest, most sophisticated telescopes on the planet. The only brown patch of earth that is visible from the moon, Atacama is sparsely populated. But you can often see women walking and digging up the terrain in a ceaseless, yet often unrewarded, search for the remains of their loved ones.

They are the mothers and wives of the country's disappeared.

Chile's Edenic period was disrupted first by the revolutionary ferment of Salvador Allende, and then, far more brutally, on Sept. 11, 1973. That was the day that Gen. Augusto Pinochet overthrew the Allende government and ushered in a 17-year reign of terror, death and destruction.

The barbarity of Pinochet's regime appeared knew no limits.

Not only did the dictatorship disappear thousands of people, taking them in the middle of the night, holding them in concentration camps, then torturing and raping them before killing them. They also deliberately buried the bones in different locations to where they had killed their victims so that the loved ones would not find them. In many cases they dumped them in the sea.

In the film, Guzmán brings together the common threads between his childhood memories, the country's premier location for astronomers, the quest of archaeologists to understand the nation's pre-Colombian past, and the unhealed wounds so many Chileans suffered during the Pinochet era.

The work starts slowly, as a massive telescope being unfurled is the only character in the film for close to the first five minutes. The pace continues in a similar vein throughout the work.

The first third or so of the work is dedicated to astronomers and archaeologists, both of whom make the point that we are always living in, and they are always studying, the past. One astronomer points out that even the perception of the present is in the very recent past because of the minute delay in thoughts moving to being consciously understood.

Guzmán moves from this metaphysical premise to pointing out the irony in Chile being such an ideal place to study the past for these two disciplines because it has yet to fully confront its own most recent history. (He also makes the point in the film that atrocities against indigenous people occurred in the 19th century as well.)

More characters enter *Nostalgia* at this point, and the film, like a boa constrictor, starts to take deeper hold of the viewer's attention and emotions.

Guzmán introduces us to an imprisoned architect who memorized every detail of the dimensions of the concentration camp in which he was imprisoned once he was in exile in Denmark. Guzmán notes that in a way the man, who is driven to remember, and his wife, who is losing her memory as she falls into the grip of Alzheimer's, are a metaphor.

We meet another former concentration camp survivor who was part of a group of about two dozen prisoners who did their own stargazing while incarcerated. Led by a doctor who knew a lot about astronomy, the group was eventually stopped by the authorities who feared they would seek to escape.

The gentleman explains that he did not escape, but did feel at those moments very free.

Guzmán also introduces us to the women and their ceaseless searches, explaining that cities all over the nation have people conducting similar searches. Sometimes, having "success" is not enough. In one of the movie's most moving scenes, a woman explains that receiving just a part of her child's body does not quiet the ache inside of her.

"He was whole when they took him," she says, tears coming to her eyes as she sits in the desert where she has spent countless hours. "I don't want just a piece of him."

Nostalgia has moments of light, too.

One of these comes in the form of an astronomer who was raised by her grandparents after her parents were detained and killed. She explains that her grandparents, who sit wordlessly on a couch, were pressured relentlessly by the government to reveal their children's location lest their granddaughter be killed.

Eventually, they relented.

Despite living with this unthinkable burden, they managed to raise her in a joyful environment. Though she thinks of herself as damaged, she sees that the son she is raising is psychologically healthy, as is her husband. This knowledge is a source of solace.

But so too is her study of astronomy and the way she has used her understanding of the natural world to formulate an attitude toward her parents' death as part of the natural course of events. Seeing this way, she says, allows her to diminish some of the pain she still feels over their death and absence from her life.

In the end, Guzmán returns to the purity of his childhood—a period that he represents through the marbles he carried around as a boy—and the lights and stars twinkling over Santiago, the nation's capital.

As the man-made lights start to go out and just the sounds remain, continuing as the credits roll, we are left with a deeper sense of the thread of seeking to answer questions from the past that connect so many in this injured, blood-soaked land.

Guzmán is a Chilean who is seeking both to share and better understand his own experience as well as to help his countrymen confront what they together have not had the courage to completely face. Yet, in this very effort, we are also left with the unsettling realization that, as Martha Minow wrote in the introduction to her work *Between Vengeance and Forgiveness*, there can be no final closure.

But we must do something.

Guzmán has given us that in his film.

Sebastián Lelio's *Gloria*

Posted on August 15, 2013

Of the many concerns that crop up when one is divorced in late middle age, one of the most basic is how to fill the days and nights previously occupied by children and spouse.

Simply put, you've got an awful lot of time, and need to figure out what to do with it. How Gloria Cumplido, the protagonist of Sebastián Lelio's movie *Gloria*, manages this challenge provides the narrative spine of this charming film.

It took Dunreith and me two times to find the Centro Arte Alameda near Baquedano, and the movie was well worth the effort for reasons that include and go beyond my learning that Umberto Tozzi, not Laura Branigan, was the first artist to sing the internationally popular song of the title.

The movie, which debuted to considerable acclaim at the Berlin Film Festival earlier this year, tells the story of Gloria, a vivacious 58-year-old divorcee who lives in Santiago and who is coming to terms with the emptiness in her life caused by her husband leaving her for a younger woman and her son and daughter moving onto the next stage of their lives.

Her son, who has sired Gloria's sole grandchild, acts utterly disinterested in her, while her daughter is leaving the country for Sweden to bear the child of her mountain-climbing boyfriend.

Neither has as much contact with Gloria as she would like. In one early scene, she calls both of her children from her work, urging them both to call her and ending by reminding them, "Yo soy tu madre".

I am your mother.

The gap left by the change in these relationships constitutes just one part of Gloria's angst. Her job appears to bore her. Her upstairs neighbor regularly stays up late, doling out verbal and physical abuse to his wife. Perhaps most troubling, Gloria's body is starting to register some of the effects of age.

She dies her hair a dark chestnut and is told by her opthamologist that her failing eyesight requires her to put in eye drops every day.

Her response to fill the void is to go to singles clubs, where she dances to 80s era tunes and seeks comfort in men's arms. This generally leads to disappointment, even as her pleasure in music is evident from the beginning of the film. (Some of my favorite moments in the movie occurred as Gloria sang along to the pop songs she listened to on her car radio while driving by herself. The film's soundtrack is consistently entertaining.)

Soon Gloria meets Rodolfo, a 65-year-old former naval officer turned entertainment park owner who says he is looking to "change things" in his life. Beyond the physical fireworks, she finds herself grateful for the attention he showers on her—she starts crying when he reads a poem declaring his passion for her—and by the emotional intimacy they begin to share with each other.

She starts to envision their having a more serious relationship, and, perhaps, a lasting commitment to each other.

This is where things get complicated.

The reality of Rodolfo's separation from his wife, and particularly his daughters, who, like Gloria's children, are 27 and 31, is murky. The daughters call him constantly, taking him away from Gloria. Yet he refuses to introduce Gloria to them, saying he does not want to subject her to them.

Gloria has her own difficulties.

She brings Rodolfo to her son's birthday party, but scarcely pays attention to him. Instead, she spends much more time drinking and looking at old family photos, including wedding pictures with her increasingly drunker husband. Rodolfo leaves without telling her or anyone else, then starts calling obsessively to explain his actions to her.

The relationship between the two lovers plays out in this turbulent and fitful manner, and the larger journey within the film is Gloria's quest to find sufficiency within herself as well as a greater acceptance of the new stage in which she finds herself.

Chilean actress Paulina García delivers a bravura performance as Gloria. Her ability to convey her character's longing, desire, impishness, joy, pain and desperation with equal dexterity both sustain the viewer's interest throughout the film and lends the somewhat predictably upbeat ending a measure of satisfaction.

García reveals Gloria's character in small moments such as how Gloria continues to look toward the terminal her daughter forbids her to enter when the daughter is flying to Sweden, how she zestfully rips off the girdle that Rodolfo wears even after his fat-reduction surgery, how she hugs her son extra long at the front door of his apartment while Rodolfo stands there, a bottle of wine in hand, or how she dances tentatively at the beginning of the film's final scene.

These gestures combine with Gloria's many activities to give her sense of hard-earned awareness and greater level of inner peace a realistic and heartwarming feeling. (At different points she tries yoga, does a bungee jump, and smokes a stash of marijuana the abusive neighbor accidentally leaves on her front doorstep. In one of the film's most painful moments, she calls her maid to fetch her after Rodolfo abandons her again.)

A film of modest scope, *Gloria* does not ask big questions.

But it does show, in an engaging way, that while Gloria may not have figured out by the film's end what to do with all the time she has at her disposal, she has stopped looking exclusively for the answer in spending time with others.

Los 80 Helps Chile Confront its Past

Posted on September 30, 2013

There are many ways to confront a nation's painful past.

With official dates of remembrances and honoring those who have died.

With statues and other types of memorials, like the one erected in honor of assassinated Chilean Senator Jaime Guzmán that Dunreith and I passed Sunday during our walk through the neighborhood of Las Condes.

Or with weighty tomes produced by prominent writers like Nobel Prize winning-author Gunter Grass, who penned *A Broad Field*, a novel about German reunification.

These methods each have their merits, and there are others that arguably have a more widespread impact.

Like Wolfgang Becker's *Goodbye Lenin*, a film about the waning days of the Communist era. The movie, which rapidly attained cult status in Germany, uses humor from start to finish as it evokes the nostalgia many East Germans felt for certain aspects of life under the regime.

Here in Chile, Andrés Wood takes the nation back to the dark days of the Pinochet dictatorship through the lens of a single family in the television series, *Los 80*, or *The 80s*.

Dunreith and I just finished watching the first season—she's shifted to make the show, rather than the original version of *Ugly Betty*, one of her major Spanish-language learning tools—and it's riveting stuff.

Wood was born in 1965, and came of age during the turbulent 1980s. His effort to represent the period with meticulous fidelity is one of the show's central commitments. Actual footage from television shows featuring presenters like the omnipresent Mario Kreutzberger, better known as Don Francisco, appear in every episode. So, too, does music from the period like *Eres*, which also appeared in Sebastián Lelio's whimsical movie, *Gloria*.

The radio programs, the expressions, the method of dress, and, I am sure, many other elements to which I am not attuned, place the viewer in 1982 as the show opens, and then moves through the decade in subsequent seasons.

Wood trains his camera on the Herreras, a middle-class family consisting of the happily married Juan and Ana, their teenage children Claudia and Martin, and their younger boy Félix. At the beginning of the first season, life is humming along in a comfortable and predictable rhythm.

Juan is a respected worker at the factory where he's been employed for many years. Ana tends the home with loving care. Claudia and Martin are studying to pursue their dreams of attending medical and aviation school, respectively. Everyone dotes on Félix.

After receiving a promotion and the higher salary that goes with it, Juan stretches and buys a color television, much to the delight of the other family members. But then he's laid off along with all of the other workers during the recession that hit the nation extraordinarily hard.

Part of the skill and appeal of Wood's show is the way he shows the impact of larger social forces and events on the family—dear friend and wise soul Ava Kadishson Schieber has talked before about always knowing that she was a pawn in the chessboard of life—without being too heavy-handed.

Juan's inability to provide for his family prompts Ana to seek work of her own—a decision that provokes fierce resistance from her unemployed husband. Wood depicts Juan's shame and helplessness at being unable to fulfill what he sees as his male responsibilities without announcing, "I'm looking at gender attitudes, people."

One of the season's more touching moments comes when Juan starts crying while talking to his father-in-law, who during his visit for Fiestas Patrias is insisting on having meat that Juan cannot afford.

There are many such instances during the show. They work because of the deep love that the family members feel for each other, even as the peaceful veneer they have managed to maintain is being ripped asunder by the events that are starting to overtake the nation. Juan's insistence that "we don't talk about money or politics" at the dinner table becomes harder to sustain as Martin joins the Air Force and Claudia finds herself drawn into left-wing politics at the University of Chile.

This attitude, as friends Miguel Huerta, Matias Torre, and Macarena Rodriguez discussed on Friday night, is at once a coping mechanism, a means to not confront the extent of the brutality that was occurring and a response to an environment in which you could be taken away for no reason, at any time. In one of the season's darker episodes, Juan experiences this terror when he speaks up for a more politically active co-worker who is being beaten relentlessly by police officers while Juan is forced to sit in the back seat of the police car.

At the same time, Wood also succeeds in creating a feeling of community that permeates the show. Everyone shops at the local store run by a fervent Pinochetista who nevertheless displays concern for Ana when Claudia is detained after a protest. Martin's fumbling first courtship, Félix's hesitation to dance the cueca and failure to convert a penalty, and Claudia's conversations with her mother about sex all are part of family life that occur in countries across the planet.

This interspersing of the ordinary concerns of family life with the increasingly ruptured tranquility in which they have been living gives the show additional potency. We care about the characters because we can relate to them, even as we understand the ways in which their lives are slowly, but steadily, being upended.

This is not to say that *Los 80* is without blemishes.

The issues in the episodes occasionally resolve too neatly in a single hour. (Items introduced in the beginning of an episode nearly always factor in at the end.) Several of the key characters are one-dimensional, and thus veer close at times to appearing like vehicles for Wood's clear anti-dictatorship perspective or his storytelling objectives.

These are but small points, though, in a potent, provocative and stimulating series that we'll continue to watch with enthusiasm.

Chileans have been doing the same.

Dunreith reported that her bringing up the show during the English conversation class we are teaching at UDP's American Corner sparked a lively and vigorous debate about life during the dictatorship. Conversations like these reached unprecedented levels this month, which contained the fortieth anniversary of the Pinochet coup.

We'll start Season Two tomorrow.

The healing throughout the country is ongoing.

The 25th Anniversary of "No"

Posted on October 8, 2013

Exactly 25 years ago, Chileans across the country, from Arica to Punta Arenas, went to the polls.

There was a single question on the ballot with just two choices: Yes or No.

The former meant a vote for continuing the 15-year reign of Gen. Augusto Pinochet Ugarte. The latter signaled a vote to end his hold on power that had begun on Sept. 11, 1973, when military forces loyal to him bombed the presidential palace, La Moneda, on the way to overthrowing democratically-elected Socialist President Salvador Allende.

The month leading up to the decision is the subject of Pablo Larraín's film *No*, which Dunreith and I watched last night at colleague and friend Andrea Insunza's recommendation.

In the movie, Gael García Bernal plays René Saavedra, the skateboard-riding, single father and advertising consultant who is a fictional composite of a number of people who were charged with designing the No campaign's advertising strategy. (In a concession to international pressure, the regime gave the No and Yes sides 15 minutes each per night on television in the 27 days leading up to the vote.)

It's been a season of anniversaries of major events in Chilean history since we've been here. Last month marked four decades since the Pinochet-led coup. A central theme of the volcanic eruption of memory-related activity around the coup anniversaries has been the assertion of "Nunca más."

Never again.

In a speech she gave at the Museum of Memory and Human Rights shortly before the anniversary day itself, torture survivor, former president and current presidential front runner Michelle Bachelet explained what the idea of "Nunca más" meant to her. In her passionate comments, Bachelet spoke about ending the climate of fear and terror that pervaded life in Chile under Pinochet and instead creating one in which human rights are respected and where there is justice.

Under Pinochet, as friend and fellow journalist Miguel Huerta said, anything could happen to you or your families at any moment, for no reason at all.

No attempts to represent that climate.

As the positive and forward-looking message of the campaign starts to resonate with the electorate—a significant portion of the film depicts Saveedra's efforts to pitch, and then film, the segment that announces "Happiness is coming"—the rattled leadership starts to stalk and threaten members of the No team. Saveedra, who places his son with his more-radical ex-wife Veronica in an effort to protect him, is one of them.

In an arc that is reminiscent of Liam Neeson's Oskar Schindler, director Larraín shows Saavedra's gradually deeper emotional involvement in the No cause as he comes into closer contact with the government's abusive practices. This puts him in increasing conflict with Lucho Guzmán, played by Alfredo Castro, his former boss and the man who eventually heads the opposite campaign.

Larraín intersperses actual footage from the era as he traces Saavedra's evolution and growth and as he leads the viewer toward the seemingly inevitable conclusion. This includes a clip of General Fernando Matthei being interviewed by media shortly before he entered the building that is now called the Gabriela Mistral Center the evening of the vote.

A member of the junta, Matthei, the father of one of Bachelet's leading opponents, said it was clear that the No side had won. His words delivered the message that the generals were abandoning their leader, who had been conspiring to devise a way to invalidate his defeat. They endorsed the triumph of democracy and the rule of law.

This moment, the ensuing celebrations among incredulous and jubilant Chileans, and the subsequent election of Patricio Aylwin as Chile's first post-dictatorship president give *No* an uplifiting feel.

Indeed, one of the film's final images shows real footage of Aylwin being installed as president. He shakes hands with Pinochet, who moves away to give the new leader his moment—an image that conveys that indeed the work of the campaign had been accomplished and that a peaceful transfer of power had been reinstated in the once-peaceful nation.

While technically true, the democracy had major caveats.

Pinochet remained the head of the military and an unelected Senator for Life who not only cast a large shadow over the nation, but never was called to legal account for the tortures, disappearances and murders that happened during his bloody tenure.

Cultural critic Nelly Richard took the film to task for much more than its uplifting ending in a lecture she delivered during a pre-anniversary symposium held at Diego Portales University. In a systematic demolition of the movie, Richard went point by point over what she felt were its many and fundamental flaws.

Among the most important: its focus on the fictional Saavedra elevates and glamorizes the role he and other advertising strategists played at the expense of organic, long-standing and independent-minded social movements.

Richard also took aim at Larraín's use of video footage from the era, saying that doing so both staked an unearned claim to historical accuracy and authenticity and, ironically, whitewashed the true terror so many Chileans experienced during that time.

This is not unfamiliar territory for critics evaluating films that tackle historic subjects. Indeed, a central aspect of some studies of Holocaust literature, art and film start with the premise that it is impossible to fully convey what literature scholar Larry Langer called the "terror and dread" experienced by people who lived through the time. There is a also a school of thought that says that the standard for critical scrutiny rises with the perceived intentions of the director.

At the same time, I would suggest that it is worth considering a study that former priest, author, and columnist James Carroll did for Harvard's Shorenstein Center.

Carroll studied the amount of coverage about the Holocaust in the United States over time, finding that there were three distinct points in which the volume of coverage spiked.

The first was in 1961, and coincided with the trial of captured Nazi Adolf Eichmann in Jerusalem.

The second occurred in 1978, and was connected with the showing of the six-part miniseries, *Holocaust* that starred, among other people, a young Meryl Streep and James Woods.

And the third took place in 1993, when *Schindler's List* debuted.

I mentioned the study's results to Richard after her lecture. Was there no value, I asked, in the popular introduction of a topic that, while not as hard-hitting as it could have been, nevertheless brought the No campaign to an audience that would otherwise know nothing about it?

Richard agreed and disagreed.

"I am not saying that there is no value to the film," she told me, before adding that she found the international response to the film very complacent and uncritical.

Here in Chile, the marking of the anniversary of the No vote was muted.

I found a thin front-page story in La Segunda that cast a positive light on the role Christian Democrats played in the campaign. Friend and memory scholar Hugo Rojas sent me the link to a piece the BBC did about the campaign. Ricardo Lagos' stern, finger-wagging statement on television that called Pinochet to account for his regime's brutality is identified as one of three key aspects of the campaign. The BBC article also speaks about the role that television played during the ultimately successful campaign.

In all, coverage of the event paled in comparison with the deluge around the coup anniversary.

Still and yet, the day provides a useful opportunity to look into the reality behind the campaign and vote represented in Larraín's movie. It also is a moment in which we can assess both how far the nation has come since the dark days of the Pinochet regime as well as how far it has yet to go to become a country whose lived reality for all matches its lofty ideals and promises to its citizens.

First Day Teaching Jitters

Posted on August 5, 2013

The first day butterflies never really go away.

I first taught nearly 30 years ago, at Bellehaven Child Development Center in East Menlo Park. Four afternoons a week during my sophomore year at college I mounted my bike and pumped away from Stanford's red stucco buildings and palm-tree laced roads. Ideals of social justice, a desire to erase my white privilege, and a burgeoning love of working with children propelled me.

I biked across the bridge that ran over Route 101, past the adolescent boys on Terminal Avenue who lazily threw rocks at me, and arrived at the center.

Silence greeted me.

Hands outstretched or folded neatly underneath one of their cheeks, the 30 children looked like sleeping angels. Their skin tones ranged from mocha to copper to dark black. The window shades draped the room in darkness.

Willie, a bass-voiced childhood friend of Grateful Dead guitarist Bob Weir, and Winetta, a hefty single mother whose ferocity masked her affection for the children, were the teachers. They circulated throughout the room, rousing the children from their post-lunch naps.

The three- to five-year olds stood up like newborn foals. Clearing the crusts from their eyes, they stretched their arms above their heads in a continuous fluid movement. They pulled their cots to Winetta, who stacked them in neat rows of ten, and assembled in a circle on the brown rug in the center of the room.

Willie turned on the record player and placed the needle delicately on the album. The sounds of Michael Jackson's *Thriller* filled the room. Myisha, Shawneequa and the rest of the children clapped for each other as each of them took their turn in the middle of the carpet.

Michael was their favorite. Twirling and break dancing with a vengeance, his signature move was a 360-degree knee spin. He yielded the floor only after Willie insisted.

I stood at the edge of the circle, transfixed. I did not ask questions about their family's incomes. Nor did I wonder why only two of the children ever had fathers pick them up, or why the kids wore the same clothes day after day and sometimes smelled unwashed.

I just knew that I was where I belonged, in a place where my values and the people I was spending time with and the pleasure in being with the children all converged.

Yet as much as I enjoyed being among the children, I also felt nervous the first time I moved from observing to leading a group.

I felt nerves two years later, when I took over a lesson for Paul Tamburello, my fourth grade and mentor teacher, and when I handled recess duty on my own.

I felt them in the fall of 1989, when I strode around the empty room of desks at Newton North High School, where I did my student teaching,

My stomach tingled with nervous anticipation in August 1992, when I arranged the chairs in my first classroom as a full-time teacher at Brown Middle School in Newton.

The same sensation filled me in August 1995, when I prepared to teach students at the Uthongathi School in Tongaat, South Africa, in the fall of 1997, before I gave my initial session for Facing History and Ourselves, and in the summer of 2001, as I got ready to teach at Longmeadow High School in Western Massachusetts.

A dozen years later, those nerves are still there.

Tomorrow, I'll teach my first class in Data Journalism at Diego Portales University.

The class will be different from the others that I've given in that it'll be in Spanish.

That's a minor source of anxiety, and I know both that I can communicate well enough and will make some grammatical errors.

On the most basic level, my nerves are a combination of caring, insecurity, and belief in education's mission, of wanting very much to make a difference in the students' lives and wondering if I'll be able to do just that.

In a commentary he wrote for the Brookline Tab and later read on public radio station WBUR before the beginning of his final year of teaching at Pierce School, Paul Tamburello wrote the following:

> *"How did the years go by so swiftly, how much have*
> *I accomplished, what's my place in the pantheon of my school's*
> *history? More importantly what's my place in the personal pantheons*
> *of the hundreds of fourth graders whom I've taught, advised,*
> *disciplined, and eaten lunch with for the past 33 years?"*

For me, the questions are slightly different as I´ve moved in the past decade away from full-time teaching and more and more into writing. But the wondering what dent we´ve had and will make on the world through our students is the same.

While it helps to know that we´ve delivered the goods before, each group is a separate adventure, with new actors and as yet unknown challenges.

At 3:30 p.m. the students will file in and take their seats.

Standing in front of them, full of hope, belief and, yes, some nerves, I´ll be there, too.

Zorba the Greek and My Data Journalism Class

Posted on August 9, 2013

My Data Journalism class with Maca Rodriguez, far left,
and Alvaro Graves, third from right.
(Photo courtesy of Jeff Kelly Lowenstein)

I read Nikos Kazantzakis' *Zorba the Greek* when I was a sophomore in college, and many of the book's moments are with me still.

I remember an old man reprimanding the narrator, also known as the bookworm, when he asks what dish is his favorite, telling him it is a great sin to say this meal is good and this meal is bad because there are people in the world who are hungry.

I think about the description of Zorba reaching out his huge hand closing his mistress Boubalina's eyes with "indescribable tenderness" after she died.

I remember Zorba's seizing of life at every possible instant, his not taking offense when Boubalina's parrot calls him by a different name, and, of course, his love of dance.

Yet one of the strongest memories of the book is when Zorba comes across an old man who is planting an almond tree. When Zorba expresses skepticism that the man will live to ever see a single almond, he tells Zorba that he acts as if he will live forever—a statement that elicits Zorba's retort that he lives every day as if it is his last.

"Two equally steep and bold paths may lead to the same peak," Kazantzakis writes.

I thought of the Greek legend's words on Thursday, when friend, lawyer and professor Macarena Rodriguez and cognitive science doctoral student Alvaro Graves came and presented to the students in my Data Journalism class at Diego Portales University.

We're just two classes into the semester at Diego Portales University, and I can already tell we're going to have a lot of fun.

I explained that there are four major ways to acquire data: writing a freedom of information request; scraping data from websites by writing code and transferring them into a format that can easily be analyzed; downloading existing data; and building a dataset.

Like the old man and Zorba in Kazantzakis' book, Macarena and Alvaro came to talk about the first two options.

Maca spoke first, explaining to the students the origin and key elements of the country's landmark 2009 transparency legislation.

"There's no greater disinfectant than sunlight," one of the slides said.

Macarena proceeded to explain why.

She put Chile's law in the context of the move by governments around the world over the last 62 years to institute similar legislation. Finland and Sweden were first in 1951, the United States followed in 1966. Maca also showed a slide of a 2011 world map of the world that indicated by country the states of national transparency laws. (Northern and Central Africa, parts of the Middle East and Asia had the biggest holes.)

Although 11 Latin American nations have freedom of information legislation, she talked the students through the history of secrecy that has shrouded many of the countries before going on to talk about key features of the Chilean law like the transparency council that decides on individual requests.

The students peppered her with questions about the council's composition and the types of records that are subject to the law.

Although the volume of questions meant we did not have time to see the sample of a successful information request that Maca had, she has agreed to look at the students' letters to help refine and make them as precise as possible.

Precision is a critical part of scraping, and Alvaro talked the students through what he and other members of the winning team accomplished in a recent scrapeathon here in Santiago. (For those who don't know, a scrapeathon is when teams compete in a specific amount of time to pull data from a publicly available site, organize them into an analyzable file and then build some sort of visualization from it.)

Alvaro and his team were interested in looking at school quality in Santiago. They used the SIMCE, a single number published by the Chilean government that ranges from 200 at the lowest to 300 at the highest. After pulling the data, the team then merged that information with geographic location and plotted the points on a map using a free tool from Google.

They then moved to show the amount of distance students would have to travel and money parents would have to pay by neighborhood to go to schools of varying quality levels. The point, unsurprisingly, was that parents in poor neighborhoods would have to pay more and have their children travel farther to have their students attend high-quality schools than their wealthier counterparts.

Again, the students lobbed a series of probing questions at Alvaro.

"How did you know where in the neighborhood people live?" one student wanted to know.

Alvaro explained that he and the team had scraped the data, joined it and built the site in eight hours, adding that the code they used was open source and available on their Github repository.

"The team plans to refine the project," he said.

Time was running very short.

I reminded the students that while we were going to hear from many American journalists during the course, we were starting with Chilean professionals who had studied in Chile and the United States who were available to them as resources and who are in different ways committed to bring the truth about their society to light.

I also repeated that the students' assignment was to write a 500-word analysis of the advantages and disadvantages of each method of data acquisition.

One of the students who had taken notes for the class said they were about 500 words and asked if he could be exempt from the essay.

No.

I took a few pictures of the speakers and students. Maca zipped out of the door and onto her next task. Alvaro lingered for a while. Several students asked again to clarify the homework.

Writing freedom of information requests and scraping data may not be the stuff of life and death that Kazantzakis wrote about in his epic novel, but they are indeed different paths to reach the same goal.

On Tuesday we'll see where the students land.

We'll tally their arguments into a list in a Google Spreadsheet, thereby showing them how to build a database.

I can't wait.

On My Own and My Students' Names

Posted on August 14, 2013

This invitation illustrates how Lowenstein is often dropped
from my name here.
(Photo courtesy of Jeff Kelly Lowenstein)

On September 4, 2000, standing underneath a tree with three branches that came together at the base, Dunreith and I held hands with our son Aidan in a circle. Guided by Justice of the Peace Bruce Zeitler, we said the marriage vows we had written to each other.

This marked the end of a Labor Day weekend in which I had moved, left a teaching career, and become both a husband and father.

Shortly thereafter, Dunreith and I began the process to legally change our names.

It was a negotiated settlement.

I initially broached the topic by suggesting that, rather than having different last names, we all have the same surname.

My choice: Lowenstein.

This idea didn't sit particularly well with my wife, who barely needed to hear the proposal before firing back that she had had her name longer, so that I should be the one, if anyone, to change. She made the additional point that Aidan also was a Kelly, so there were in effect two of them and one of me.

Despite this decidedly unpromising beginning to the conversation, we eventually came to agree on, and embrace, the name Kelly Lowenstein.

We liked the flow of Dunreith's name going before mine over the reverse, agreed that we didn't like the idea of a hyphen and felt more comfortable using both of our names rather than coming up with a hybrid like "Kellstein" or "Lowelly."

We made the change official by having our Social Security cards reflect the combination name we had chosen.

This ushered in the beginning of countless discussions with administrators, school officials, receptionists at doctor's offices, people in payroll and billing departments, and pharmacists, just to name a few.

The conversation usually involves the following steps.

We are asked our last name.

We give it, explaining that there are two words, Kelly and Lowenstein, with no hyphen in between them.

The person in front of us or on the other end of the phone line concludes that our last name is either Kelly or Lowenstein.

We repeat our original statement.

I often add that I took Dunreith's name, which was Kelly, while she took Lowenstein, so that together our last name is Kelly Lowenstein.

The person appears to understand, and then asks if we have a hyphen in our name.

We say again that we do not.

Although this may seem like an enormously tedious and time-consuming experience, it can have certain advantages in journalism. In my experience, the vast majority of administrative assistants have been women. I've found that telling them about having taken Dunreith's name elicits one of two reactions.

"That's interesting" or "That's different" is the first. The emotion behind this response can range from intrigued to skeptical.

The second response happens more frequently.

Much more enthusiastic, it includes statements like "That's sweet" or "I've got to talk to my husband about that."

The point for me as a journalist is my hope that the goodwill indicated by the second response will lead to my message being passed along with more alacrity. I don't have any data to prove this actually happens, but it certainly feels that way.

In this context, then, an additional reason for my being excited to travel to Chile was the fact that folks go by two unhyphenated last names here.

For those who don't know, people generally have their father's last name in the place where the Kelly is for us, while their mother's surname goes where the Lowenstein does.

I will say that the attendance sheet I received from Diego Portales University for the Data Journalism course I'm offering gave me pause as the majority of the students were listed as having four names.

For example, what would you think a student named "Doren Jara Lowry Sebastián" would be called?

If you said, "Lowry Doren," with Lowry being his first name, you were ahead of me. By at least two, if not three, steps.

My confusion was not aided by the fact of our having two Oscars—the first one on the sheet is "Delbene Peñaloza Oscar Felipe", while the second is "Pacheco Castillo Oscar Walter"—or that several of the students have three names.

Then there's Rafael.

He was not on the sheet at all, but wrote down that his name was "Rafael Martínez."

But when he sent me his email, it said that his name is "Rafael Martínez Carvallo."

Throw in the additional factor that just three of the students have attended all of the classes, and I don't mind saying that it's been a bit of a struggle for me to get my head around the whole issue.

Over time, though, a pattern emerged.

If there are four names on the register, the first of the four is the father's last name and the one that the student uses. The third name is typically the student's first name, while the fourth name is the student's middle name.

In other words, "Aburto Miranda Katherinee Alejandra" is "Katherinee Aburto."

"Araya Marambio Hernán Felipe" goes by "Hernán Araya."

And so on.

My understanding of my students' names has had an accompanying revelation.

Even though most of them have a pair of unhyphenated names, they and other folks at the university don't look at my last name and think that it is Kelly Lowenstein.

Quite the opposite, in fact.

On professional invitations, name tags for presentations and students greeting me in the hallways, a consistent name rings out.

Jeff Kelly.

Dunreith loves it.

I don't mind, either, even if I do feel a twinge of disappointment at the knowledge that the end of explaining our name choice has not been as imminent as I had first hoped after arriving.

Students Progressing in Data Journalism Class, Channeling Paul Tamburello

Posted on October 29, 2013

I love to teach.

It's a passion that stretches across three decades and the past millennium back to high school, when I thought it would be fun to be a teacher someday and spoke to teachers about what they did and why they did it.

In 1985 I worked with three- to five-year-olds four days a week at the Bellehaven Child Development Center in East Menlo Park, California. I only was there for a quarter, but it was long enough for me to feel that I was where I belonged.

The following year, after my parents were in a near-fatal car accident, I returned home to be with my family in Brookline, Massachusetts. Pierce School Principal Al Fortune invited me into his office, expressed his concern in a surprisingly quiet tone and offered me a job as a recess aide. Touched by his gesture, I accepted on the spot.

I only learned later that the reason the job was open was because the previous recess aide had fled her post after having been pushed into the snow and pelted with snowballs by members of the eighth grade class who were labeled by adults throughout the building as "the worst class in 30 years."

The eighth graders were as advertised, eyes glittering with malice and the knowledge that they had toppled the last authority figure. Nevertheless, I loved working with them and the rest of the grades.

After graduating from Stanford, I returned to Pierce for my most formative teaching apprenticeship: a two-year stint in my fourth grade teacher Paul Tamburello's classroom—the same room where I had been a student a dozen years earlier. To this day I still draw on the lessons I learned in Paul's laboratory of teaching excellence.

He taught me how to help students chart their progress, and how to cultivate a healthy sense of dramatic occasion and humor even as you're pushing the students beyond the limits of what they think is possible.

He showed me how and when to be firm, and how you can at times win by losing. The more power you give out, the more power you get back, he would say.

Paul continually displayed an organic sense of learning, creating whole units from a student's comment that reinforced essential skills while showing his charges that they could follow their curiosity wherever it led. Above all, Paul demonstrated over and over again the importance of witness, tenacity and perspective.

I've applied those lessons in the quarter century since I finished what he called my "post-graduate degree in fourth grade." Most recently, that has taken place in my Data Journalism classroom here at Diego Portales University in Santiago.

It took a while to sort out exactly who on the roster actually would attend the class on a regular basis, but we've gotten there.

It also has taken me a couple of months to fully understand the implication of the Chilean university system for students' attendance and delivery of the assignments I've given them.

As opposed to the United States, where students take anywhere from three to five classes, here students take as many as eight or nine classes. This has all kinds of academic consequences for them, not the least of which is that they calculate exactly how many classes they need to make to reach the 60 percent departmental requirement to pass the course.

I've adjusted to this environment by assigning three cumulative projects throughout the semester, by working to make the class as stimulating as possible, to alternate between exhorting the students to attend and noting their absence, and, at base, to accept whoever comes that day as the lineup we have to work with for that session.

As Paul did throughout his teaching career, I've worked to link what we do in the class to the larger world. I do this so that students understand why they are learning what we are doing and so that they have tangible examples of where they can go.

Like Paul, I bring in guest speakers to expose students to the community of people throughout the world who share our love of data.

Today, the invitado, or guest, was Joe Germuska, a former history major from Northwestern who played a key role in the development of the *Chicago Tribune's* NewsApps team, and who has been, since December, working at Northwestern University's Knight Lab. This interdisciplinary space seeks to help advance news media innovation through exploration and experimentation.

He also helped me get here by introducing me at the June 2012 Investigative Reporters and Editors conference to Miguel Paz, the founder of Poderopedia, a site that traces relationships between Chilean elites. Miguel connected me to Carlos Aldunate, who wrote me the letter of invitation that was a requirement for becoming a Fulbright scholar.

Joe told the students about his background, talked them through a number of projects he had helped develop like the *Chicago Tribune's* crime site and CensusReporter.org, a tool he worked on that tries to make Census data more accessible to reporters.

He talked about the importance of placing data into context and of making information as accessible as possible. He stressed an integrated approach to planning and development, saying they are related, not separate, stages.

At base, Joe emphasized the need to be skeptical, critical consumers of information and technology, and the role that programming skills can play in assisting. The students applauded Joe's comments with genuine enthusiasm.

From there we went over my visit to *La Nación*, the newspaper in Argentina I went to yesterday. I passed out stickers that members of their data team had given me.

We went over their midterm projects. I told them in general what they had done well in comparison with the first one they had completed about a month earlier. I also went over the elements I liked from each student's project.

With some it was their graphic. With others it was the map they had created. Still others wrote a fine summary, opening paragraph or conclusion. Projects' structure, writing skill and the fact of passing the work in at all each generated praise.

The students clearly understood better how to do data-oriented journalism, even if the depth of their work was not what it could be. I told them other areas where they needed to improve and shared what I would do to raise the quality of my work with them.

One thing I had not done as well as I could have was to give the students sufficient time to work on the practical tools I had shown them. So, after explaining how I was going to give them more time, I did just that. The students spent the end of class starting with the assignment.

These are all strategies I absorbed during my apprenticeship.

It's always a positive sign when students voluntarily stay beyond the scheduled time the class ends. That happened today with close to a dozen of them. And as they walked by me on the way out, they did a combination of shaking hands, exchanging high fives, or, in the Chilean custom, kissing me on the cheek.

Their eyes danced with pleasure. So did mine, both because of the progress they are making and because of the space we have created amongst us.

In this space failure is a virtue and all are accepted.

In this space we learn from each other and the best idea wins.

In this space we work to support each other.

I am deeply grateful to all those, including Joe, who have helped me be here and have this opportunity. I'm profoundly appreciative of my students for how they've engaged this new and often challenging class.

And I feel doubly blessed to have learned how to teach in Paul's class more than a quarter century ago and to still be channelling what he shared with me all these many years later.

Data Journalism Class Ends

Posted on December 12, 2013

Although generally joyous, the end of school also has a twinge of sadness. Our time together—and, with it, my chance to directly impact the students I teach—has finished.

Life goes on.

Last Tuesday marked the addition of a new group to the list of endings: the 20 or so students in my Data Journalism class at Diego Portales University.

It's been close to three decades since I first worked with three- to five-year-old students at the Bellehaven Child Development Center in East Menlo Park. I still remember their eyelashes, the angelic expressions on their sleeping faces and the silence that greeted me after I had biked away from Stanford's leafy luxury and toward their grittier neighborhoods. I didn't know what I was doing with them. I didn't know why so few fathers came to get them. But I did know that I was where I belonged.

Since then I've worked with students of all kinds of ages and backgrounds in Boston suburbs, Appalachian classrooms, and one of South Africa's first private multi-racial schools.

This group was special, though. It was both my first crop of Chilean students and my first Spanish-language class. We adjusted to each other as the semester unfolded.

I learned both how to explain the requirements with more clarity and to convey my insistence that they attend class and do work in order to pass. I changed the assignments from a series of smaller items and what amounted to a continent-wide fishing expedition around lotteries, to three projects of increasing scope, rigor and sophistication.

For their part, the students had a series of experiences—projects, articles, guest lecturers—that allowed them to better understand the sensibility

I wanted them to develop and the world of data journalism they could enter, not just the data analysis skills they needed to acquire.

But I didn't just talk to the students about data.

I told them how I had wanted to go to Chile for many years and how I had applied to the Fulbright program four times before being accepted.

I told them about how extraordinary I found what was happening in the country before the September 11 anniversary of the coup, and how significant the presidential elections were.

I also talked to them about my tremendous fortune in being there with Dunreith, and about being able to work on a project for *The New Yorker* with my brother Jon, who shared his work and talked with the students twice. I let them know how much it meant to me to have Dad there, who told them about the importance of being actively involved in both sides of a mentoring relationship.

Finally, I urged them to give themselves enough time to do the kind of work of which I knew they were capable and to finish strong.

On Tuesday, they did just that.

One by one they stood and delivered at the front of the room. They talked about their data sets, their maps, their graphics and the law they chose to evaluate, which was part of the curriculum. Using Powerpoint or Prezi or Google Docs, students who had had no idea of what a database was at the beginning of the semester explained how they had acquired and analyzed their data.

Dunreith and Aidan arrived about two thirds of the way through the class.

"My family," I said. "Please give them a round of applause."

The class complied with gusto.

The last student finished about 10 minutes after our scheduled time, and I moved forward to the front of the room for the last time. I apologized for the lateness and asked them to think back to August, when they knew little to nothing about data. I told them again how much I had enjoyed working with them and how being there and working with them was the realization of a dream for me.

I told them that I had learned that it's possible to live from dreams and values, and that I hope they felt the same way. I explained that they had had the opportunity to meet some of the people in the world who do the best work in this area.

"And your brother," one student called out.

"And your father," said another.

"You're almost there," I said. "I'm proud of the progress you've made, but you're not done yet. You can finish strong."

"I believe in you," I said. "I'm available to you as a resource now and in the future. And I'll be in my office tomorrow if you need help."

Then I thanked them and told them they could go. The students applauded and started to leave. I stood by the door.

The male students and I hugged each other on the way out.

The women and I kissed each other's cheeks.

Then it was over.

As always, I knew that I would reflect and realize that, despite my efforts, I could have done better.

Vulnerability in the knowledge, too, that life continues its ceaseless forward flow. The end of the class anticipated, in a small but real way, the ultimate ending we all face.

Drained.

But I also felt good, deep down good, at the knowledge that I had given my best, at what we had done together and at the transmission of a spark that I believe, at least for some, will not soon be extinguished.

Meeting Juan Guzmán

Posted on October 20, 2013

Judge Juan Guzmán, left, at the showing of the documentary film,
Los Muertos No Callan, in early September.
(Photo courtesy of Jeff Kelly Lowenstein)

As he deliberated over what was arguably the most important decision of his professional life, Juan Guzmán did not talk to any of his fellow judges.

To do so, he thought, would involve entering a world with all kinds of unequal levels of power and could contaminate his choice about whether to indict General Augusto Pinochet. Instead he spoke with one of his daughters. And he talked with his wife, Inés Watine.

It was 2004. The choice about whether the aging dictator, then nearly 90 years old, was fit to stand trial was a difficult one for Guzmán for two primary reasons.

The first was that he had a report from a psychiatrist that stated Pinochet had performed well enough on 15 criteria of mental acuity to be categorized as mentally intact, and therefore able to stand trial. But the report from a neurologist said exactly the opposite, stating that Pinochet had suffered too much mental deterioration to be involved in legal proceedings.

The other level was more personal and more complicated for Guzmán.

He felt compassion for Pinochet.

In him, he did not see the brutal military leader who had led the overthrow of the country's democratically-elected government and overseen 17 years of torture, terror, disappearances and murder. Instead he saw an elderly man nearing death whose physical and mental failings reminded him of his father.

Guzmán spoke with his wife, the daughter of a World War II French resistance fighter.

She asked him two critical questions.

"Would you have had compassion for Hitler during World War II?"

"Of course not," he answered about Germany's genocidal leader.

"Would you have had compassion for Stalin during World War II?"

"Even more I would not," he said, thinking about the 20 million people Stalin had been responsible for killing.

Guzmán's conflict receded. He knew what he had to do.

Guzmán told Dunreith and me this story toward the end of an interview in the law office near presidential palace La Moneda where he is working.

I had first seen the judge, who is tall and bearded and soft-spoken and gentle and respectful and impressively energetic for a man of 74 years of age, in Patricio Lanfranco's film, *The Judge and The General*, shortly before we traveled to Chile. The movie traces Guzmán's odyssey as he moved from a sheltered, right-wing cocoon to becoming a powerful instrument of justice.

I had seen him in person at a showing in the basement of the Providencia Library at Cafe of *Los Muertos No Callan*, or *The Dead Are Not Silent*. It's a German documentary film about the Pinochet regime's torture and murder of former high-ranking Allende officials like José Tohá and Orlando Letelier. Letelier's widow Isabel was in the room that evening.

Guzmán paid elegant homage to the courage she, the other widows in the film and so many women had displayed during and after the dictatorship. After that session I had approached the judge and asked for his contact information. A half-dozen emails and about a month later, Dunreith and I were sitting across a long, wooden table from him in the late afternoon.

The son of Juan Guzmán, a diplomat and famed poet, Guzmán told us about how he grew up in an unreflecting conservative environment. He attended upmarket St. George's College and the Catholic University before beginning his legal career.

In those times, he was mostly concerned with his professional advancement—an orientation that he said revealed his right-wing leanings. Infused with the political ideals of his family, he saw the Pinochet coup as necessary, but did not anticipate the barbarity the leader and his minions would inflict on the people. Guzmán made it clear that he had never attended a political demonstration, as to do so would violate his code as a judge.

Then the notice of his assignment to the Pinochet case came. Judge Guzmán didn't describe the room or the date in great detail. But he did say he understood immediately what it meant, how it would become totally consuming. He couldn't hear anything else his superior said.

Lanfranco's film shows what he did, how he ventured from the seclusion and went around the country traveling into what he called the "abyss" of the past. But it doesn't show everything.

It doesn't show all of the death threats and the political pressure he endured during the years he made his lonely journey. He didn't feel fear in a personal sense, he told us, because he thought of himself like a soldier in a cause. But he did worry about his family.

Of course, the film does not depict what he's done since the case. It doesn't inform the viewer that the one-time unreflecting right-winger has gone on to defend indigenous Mapuche people accused of terrorism.

Guzmán's decision to indict Pinochet did not ultimately land the dictator in prison. Not even for a single day. It did not narrow the chasm between the classes or end the racism and prejudice here in Chile that he said are the cause of so much indignation. Nor did it heal all of the wounds caused by the dicatorship's bloody reign.

But he did, in the moment that he had been called, respond in a way far greater than anyone had expected. He allowed himself to leave his comfortable cocoon and to confront the fact that systematic atrocities took place.

He found within himself the courage and the strength to defy the expectations of those who had appointed him to the task, to defy the political pressure and threats, and to not only go after the generals, but to go after the leader himself.

The judge said he could talk for days—a signal that indeed it was time for us to go. I said I'd be willing to listen.

Before we left, I told him that I had also learned to listen to my wife, and that good things happened when I did.

We all laughed. And as we departed, we had a sense that we had shared something special.

Journalistic legend and Chilean trailblazer John Dinges had told me about the film based on Guzmán's life and evolution before we came here in mid-July When Dunreith and I watched it, I didn't dream that I would ever meet, let alone interview, the man. But now I have.

The Metro was packed to the gills on the way home.

The light had not descended from the sky.

Hernán's Gutiérrez's Memory and Imagination

Posted on December 4, 2013

Hernán Gutiérrez stands in the chocolate shop he owns in Algarrobo.
(Photo courtesy of Jon Lowenstein/NOOR/Pulitzer Center on Crisis Reporting)

Imagine that you're in Santiago, Chile in 1973.

Imagine that you're 13 years old and walking to school with your father.

Imagine that there's been a coup in your country that deposed the president and left him dead.

Imagine that your school was closed for about a week. When you returned, many, if not most, of the teachers you worked with and learned from and loved are gone.

This included Julia Del Rosario Retamales Sepulveda. A 55-year-old Communist, she was for you the sweetest, kindest, most nurturing teacher there was. Imagine that you learn later that she was detained at Villa Grimaldi, the largest and most notorious detention center in the network of such facilities established by the DINA, Pinochet's secret police.

You never saw her again.

Imagine that you're walking along the Rio Mapocho with your father on the way to school.

You see something floating downstream.

You realize that you are seeing dead bodies.

Your father tries to protect you and stops you from moving closer.

You can't see everything, but you see enough to realize that some of the bodies have been shot.

Others have no heads.

Imagine that you walk along the river the next day.

You see more bodies.

The day after that.

Even more.

Hernán Gutiérrez does not need to imagine because this all happened to him in the fall of 1973.

"It was horrible," he said, shuddering as he described the terror inflicted on the people during the Pinochet dictatorship. Forty years later, the memories are still with him.

The trauma of what he saw has not stopped Gutiérrez from marrying and raising a family or from moving forward with business endeavors. His wife had a similar experience after the coup, so they each understand what the other experienced.

In the early 1980s, the couple moved to Germany for eight years because they did not want to raise their two boys in a society that instilled such fear in its citizens. They returned in the early 1990s, moving from Santiago's bustle to the quiet seaside town Algarrobo, where they've set up a life together.

They own a chocolate shop on the main street of Carlo Alessandri. Two doors down, she also runs a clothing store. Their sons have grown and become men. One is an artist whose work adorns the wall of the clothing store. A daughter-in-law works in the chocolate store. Life is quiet and peaceful.

But the memories still sit uneasily beneath the surface.

When he thinks about them, they remind Hernán not only of that darker, earlier time. They make him question those who were older and say they did not know.

"If I could know this at 13," he asked, "how could they not know what was happening?"

After we visited Hernán, we drove to Villa Grimaldi, the former restaurant that became a detention center during the Pinochet era, a place of unspeakable evil where people were tortured and the torturers' children played in a nearby pool.

We walked to the part of the park that honors women who were detained and disappeared there. Each woman has a plaque that looks like a multi-colored tile lollipop planted in the ground near a rose. The flowers are arranged in a series of circles.

In one of the circles, there is a tile and flower for Julia Del Rosario Retamales Sepulveda.

Just as Hernán remembered.

He does not have to imagine.

The Pulitzer Center on Crisis Reporting supported this story.

Mario Hernandez and Los Patitos

Posted on October 9, 2013

Mario Hernandez has worked at Los Patitos restaurant since 1969.
(Photo courtesy of Jeff Kelly Lowenstein)

If you work at a restaurant long enough you become part of the menu.

At least that's what has happened to Mario Hernandez.

He first started working at Los Patitos, a seafood restaurant in sleepy oceanfront Algarrobo whose name means "the ducklings," as a 16-year-old. That was in 1969. He's worked there ever since.

Don Mario served thousands and thousands of customers as his three boys grew up and became men.

He waited on poet-diplomat and Nobel prize winner Don Pablo Neruda and his third wife Matilde Urrutia. (He said the former's personality was "special", while the latter was "normal.") He took the order of Socialist President Salvador Allende. Don Mario also served military leaders during the Pinochet dictatorship—a group that he divided in two parts.

The smaller portion consisted of "good" generals like General Oscar Bonilla, who Don Mario said tried to restrain Pinochet's murderous excesses and died in a mysterious plane crash in 1975.

The larger group were "bad," he explained, shaking his head with disgust.

The dictatorship hit Don Mario's home community hard, he said. People would disappear in the middle of the night and never return. Many people. A climate of fear pervaded.

"What was it like to serve people who you knew did these terrible things," I asked?

Don Mario stared. For a minute, rather than an empty patio, it seemed as if he could see the leaders of the junta who had inflicted such massive damage on the country.

"It was work," he said, just a touch of sadness entering his voice.

He worked at Los Patitos in 1988, the year he and Chileans across the country overcame their fear, voted with their hearts and aspirations, and voted No to the dictatorship.

Five years from retirement, Mario looks younger than his 60 years. His face is youthful and unlined. His black hair is a little thin in the back and he's carrying some extra weight, but his movements are energetic and he smiles easily. We met on Sunday night, when Dunreith and I were the only customers under the awning outside the restaurant. We had initially checked the menu, gone to survey other options and returned to Los Patitos when we discovered that the nearby Peruvian and Italian restaurants were closed.

It was a little cool on the patio. Mario took a little while to warm up, too. When he did, though, the information flowed quickly and freely.

He told us about his three boys, all in their 30s now, and living and working in Santiago. He carefully pulled out the business card for the oldest from his wallet and showed it to us with reverence.

Don Mario talked about being good friends with Manuel Araya, Neruda's chauffeur whose assertions about the great poet being poisoned have contributed to his body being exhumed.

"He's talked about that for years," Don Mario said. "He told me about that for the first time in 1978. Araya said that Don Pablo got an injection in his stomach, which turned red."

"So you believe it?" I asked.

"It's the truth," he declared.

Don Mario stood to the side of us, his head jerking regularly as he spoke. Often he didn't respond to what I was saying, but kept going with his train of thought. It wasn't out of rudeness, but rather as if he didn't hear me.

He did connect when I mentioned our friend and Chilean guide Alejandra Matus.

"Alejandra Matus," he said, brightening. "I know her. That was a good book." He was referring to Alejandra's *The Black Book of Chilean Justice*, her powerful expose of the Chilean judiciary in the Pinochet era. The judge's decision the day after the book's publication in the spring of 1999 to recall all of the copies and the possibility of her serving five years in jail prompted Alejandra to flee the country. The book was banned, but that didn't stop Don Mario from getting a copy.

"My copy was photocopied in Argentina," he said, smiling. A friend from Santiago got it for him.

"I'm not a Communist, but I liked that book," he said, shedding his manner of long-time employee and leaning in close when Dunreith and I stood up to go.

"You're not a Communist, but you like to know the truth," I said.

Don Mario smiled again. "Tell her I sent my greetings," he said.

We shook hands. His grip wasn't firm, but contained genuine enthusiasm. Dunreith and I exited the patio and started to walk back to the rustic cottage in the woods where we were staying.

Mario Hernandez was there, standing vigil over the restaurant where he's worked so long that his name is a part of its history.

On Ángela Bachelet Jeria and Bearing Witness

Posted on December 11, 2013

Michelle Bachelet hugs her mother Ángela Bachelet Jeria at the Villa Grimaldi compound where they both were detained during the Pinochet dictatorship.
(Photo courtesy of Jeff Kelly Lowenstein)

Bearing witness is the call and burden of the trauma survivor, but not all choose to accept it.

Ángela Bachelet Jeria has done just that, though, for nearly 40 years.

The trained archaeologist's life was changed permanently and fundamentally by the Pinochet coup in September 1973. Her husband Alberto, an Air Force general, stayed loyal to President Salvador Allende and the Constitution. For that decision he was detained and tortured for several months. In 1974 he died of heart problems that Judge Mario Carrozo said were caused by his torture.

The death of a husband at the hands of his former comrades and friends would have been more than enough for many to bear. For Ángela Bachelet Jeria, however, her troubles were just beginning.

On January 10, 1975, along with her daughter Michelle, a popular and politically active student, she was blindfolded and taken to the notorious Villa Grimaldi compound, according to the website ThisisChile.cl. It was the largest of the network of such sites run by the DINA, or Pinochet's secret police.

Mother and daughter were separated.

Both endured interrogation and torture.

Michelle Bachelet was confined to a cell with a bunk bed with eight other female prisoners. Ángela Bachelet Jeria was held in "the tower," an infamous area within the camp that was located near a pool where the torturers' children used to play. She was kept for nearly a week without food or water.

Both women were transferred to the Cuatro Alamos detention center, where they stayed until the end of January, the website said.

After being spared death due to their connections with high-ranking military officers, the pair were released and lived in exile in Australia, and East Germany.

Dr. Jeria, the widow and torture survivor, worked from abroad to bring about the demise of the regime that had robbed her of her husband and her country of a democracy.

She has continued that fight through Pinochet's defeat in the 1988 plebiscite, through the restoration of democracy, through her daughter becoming the nation's first elected female president, and through the flurry of memory-related activity around the fortieth anniversary of the coup in September.

I first saw her at a memorial event that she attended at Villa Grimaldi in September with her daughter. The former president's emotions were visible as she wiped a tear from her eye, even as a bevy of cameras recorded her every move.

Looking fit and trim, with a full head of brown hair, Dr. Jeria seemed less visibly impacted by her latest return to the place where she had suffered so much. I had wondered what was happening within her. On Monday, I got a chance to learn the answer.

I saw Dr. Jeria, who had been erroneously introduced as the mother of the president, not ex-president, at the launch event for the 2013 annual report of the National Institute for Human Rights. Established during her daughter's term as president, the institute issues an annual review of the state of human rights in the nation.

The event had had an uneven cadence.

Director Lorena Fries had delivered a frank assessment of the problems that still remain in the country, with the treatment of indigenous people, the practice of torture on those who are incarcerated and the issue of abortion heading the list.

President Sebastián Piñera arrived late, received a copy of the report and appeared ready to head off the stage before being asked if he would like to deliver some remarks.

He pulled a sheaf of paper from a suit pocket and proceeded to deliver a nearly hour-long list of his administration's accomplishments in the area of human rights as well as his top legislative priorities. This included lengthy sections on abortion and the nation's indigenous—which just minutes before had been among the chief problems mentioned in the institute's report that he had praised and whose leader he had approved for another term.

A steady stream of whistling, heckling and banner-raising accompanied the president as he spoke. He appeared to take note of the disruption, looking up at times from his paper and raising his voice, but generally he ploughed forward, seemingly unperturbed, if not openly indifferent.

The large security men in dark suits and neatly coiffed hair seemed far more uncomfortable, looking actively torn between restoring order by forcing the offenders to leave and exercising a restraint based on their knowledge that to do so would go even more directly against the event's mission than the presidential appropriation of the stage he had been given.

Pinnera's address ground on and on before he concluded with a call for everyone to remember that they were all Chileans and should not let differences stand between them.

The applause he received was tepid at best.

Dunreith and I moved gratefully into the reception area. I secured and gulped down a wine glass full of orange juice. Then I saw Dr. Jeria. Well dressed as always, this time in a brown pants suit.

I walked over and introduced myself, explaining that Dunreith and I had been in the country for five months and that I was at the tail end of a stint as a Fulbright Scholar at Diego Portales University.

I told her that I had seen her at the Villa Grimaldi commemoration, that I admired her courage in being able to go back to the place that had been a site of such intense suffering for her.

She smiled, revealing a row of clean, white teeth that sat atop unreceded gums.

"What had that been like?" I asked.

"Unlike the concentration camps of Eastern Europe, the camps here were destroyed by the perpetrators," she explained in a smooth, deep, melodic voice. "By going to events such as the commemoration, we say that it happened and shouldn't happen again. We do this even though returning means that the memories of that dark, distant time are triggered anew." Going there meant that she had to "revivir," she said.

To live again.

I told her about our family's history in Germany, how we had lost family members in the Holocaust, but also how we had returned with Dad in May of last year. I let her know how much it meant to us that Dad had found it within himself to go back, to put himself back in that zone and time of memory and forgetting, how he did it in large part for us.

Dr. Jeria listened, nodding sagely and answering again in that even voice. For a minute I felt young and small, like I was talking to a grandmother who understood everything.

She asked me for a card and read it after I handed it to her.

More people were gathering around her to hug and embrace, to gain strength from her unbowed generosity and clarity of purpose. I caught her eye and told her it was good to meet before we left. She smiled again and we squeezed each other's hand.

Ángela Bachelet Jeria was in the process of fulfilling her duty of truth and memory for the day.

More awaited.

Viva La Mundial

Posted on October 16, 2013

The moment of victory at Paseo Orrego Luco.
(Photo courtesy of Jeff Kelly Lowenstein)

In the three months that we've been in Chile, we've seen events drenched in emotion.

We've seen the agonizing pain of surviving loved ones holding up large black and white photos of their sons, husbands, uncles, daughters, and nieces who were disappeared during the Pinochet dictatorship in the 70s and have never returned.

We've seen the exuberance of Chileans drinking Terremotos and eating anticuchos for days as they celebrated "El Dieciocho" on September 18, the national Day of Independence.

But perhaps the greatest show of feeling came last night, when the country's national soccer team punched its ticket to go to Brazil next year for the World Cup, the planet's largest sporting event.

The unifying power of sport has been commented on before.

In *Invictus*, the film based on John Carlin's book, Clint Eastwood shows how Nelson Mandela donned the once-hated green jersey of the Springbok rugby team to bring the nation together in its quest to win the Rugby World Cup the year after South Africa's first free and democratic elections.

In 1967, the great Pelé literally caused a 48-hour ceasefire in secessionist Biafra so that both sides could watch him play.

Here in Chile, the country remains deeply divided about the legacy of the Pinochet era, but there there was no apparent division within the nation last night.

The cancellation by non-profit Inria-Chile of their previously planned Data Tuesday meeting was the first sign of the game's significance.

The second came in Papi Pollo, a rotisserie chicken joint near our apartment that I go to regularly. Amidst the heat and grease of the french fries, sopaipillas and whole chickens that a man in white shirt and pants cut with impressive dexterity, the other worker, a stocky man with black hair and a round, open face, told me that he was giving all his attention to the evening's game.

He was concentrating so hard that he gave me an extra 1,000 pesos for the half chicken I was taking back to our apartment.

"You can give me this if you want," I said. "But the charge is 3,500 pesos, not 2,500. It's important to focus on the game, but you have to focus on money, too."

We laughed and shook hands after I gave him all the money.

First stop

I left our building and went out in the warm, clear evening air shortly before the game started.

I walked up Providencia Avenue, stopping at the newspaper stand that also sells candy and portraits of iconic music stars like Elvis that are hung on a fence on the other side of the sidewalk. About a dozen people had formed a half circle around the color television that had been carefully placed atop a stand so that all could see. Most were sitting, and a few were standing. I bought a coke to help establish my legitimacy and started snapping pictures.

The first 25 minutes of the game were generally in favor of Chile, whose players were wearing red shirts and who were playing in front of 67,000 fans at Estadio Nacional, the National Stadium. They were issuing full-throated roars from the moment the referee blew the whistle to start the match, which Chile only needed to tie to advance to La Mundial.

Things were quieter at the kiosk, where the group watched intently, grimacing when Ecuador threatened and holding their hands up when Chile threatened, but did not score.

But they didn't stay that way after a header by Alexis Sánchez zipped past the Ecuadorean goalkeeper and into the back of the net for a 1-0 lead. Sánchez ripped off his shirt in ecstasy.

The crowd gathered around the television didn't do that, but erupted in joy, yelling, screaming, jumping up and down and punching their fists in the air. I continued to take pictures until one of the celebrants came over and told me in English with the utmost seriousness: "Enough. Enough with the pictures. You can stay here and watch the game with us, but stop taking pictures."

So I left.

Paseo Orrego Luco

I walked further up the street, crossing over to the other side and stopping at Paseo Orrego Luco.

It's an outdoor drinking establishment enclosed on three sides by buildings and filled with tables that sit comfortably under large, tan umbrellas and beneath the light provided by yellow, red, green and orange lanterns.

Adapting a page from South Africa's hosting of the World Cup in 2010, the owner of the place, which was doing a very brisk business in french fries and beer delivered by bustling waiters, set up at least a dozen televisions of varying sizes so that everyone could easily see the action.

The crowd, many of whom were wearing red shirts and a number of whom sported jester hats with the national colors, also exploded in jubilation just as I was pulling up, when Gary Medel deposited the ball from a Sánchez header into the net for a 2-0 lead.

The margin held until halftime.

Chile played more conservative soccer to start the second half, and the game Ecuador squad pressed forward. About 20 minutes into the half, the home side surrendered a goal to Felipe Caicedo, who benefited from a lengthy run up the middle by Antonio Valencia.

The goal caused some apprehension among the multitudes at Paseo, but the hosts were never seriously threatened after that. As the minutes wore down into injury time, the chant of "Chi-Chi-Chi, Le-Le-Le, Vi-va Chi-le!" grew less anxious and increasingly confident.

So, too, did the verses of an ode to the tournament their team has never won, but was about to join.

"Oh, viva la Mundial,
la Mundial, la Mundial,
Viva la Mundial."

Long live the World Cup.

Victory Celebrations

The referee blew the final whistle and the celebrations began in earnest. Fists punched in the air.

Passionate embraces.

Flags waving.

Horns honking from passing cars.

Kids banging on the windows of the buses they were riding.

A woman in the back seat shaking her ample bosom as all around her laughed.

My camera had just about died, and I was feeling the effects of having gotten just two and a half hours of sleep, so decided to head back home. But before I did, I returned to the kiosk where I had been watching. The owner, lean and tall with at least a day's stubble and a blue sweater, was there.

"Felicidades a Chile," I said.

Congratulations to Chile.

We hugged.

I started singing the World Cup tribute song when I entered the building. The doorman, who had watched the game on television, smiled widely. I congratulated him, too, and said that Chile deserved the win.

"Ecuador was good," I said. "But Chile was better. And now they're going to the Mundial."

He agreed.

I sang the song again, raising my voice as I walked by the apartment next to us, whose residents often partied into the wee hours of the weekend.

The festivities lasted for hours.

Oh, viva la Mundial. La Mundial, La Mundial. Viva la Mundial.

The Busy Life
of Mayor Mario Gebauer

Posted on September 25, 2013

Mario Gebauer, right, Mayor of Melipilla.
(Photo courtesy of Jeff Kelly Lowenstein)

A few years ago, Mario Gebauer was planning to set aside some quiet, reflective time to study social anthropology.

But then came the call to serve in government in Santiago.

He answered.

In 2008 he decided to run for Mayor of Melipilla, a community about an hour southwest of Santiago. During his campaign Mario walked to thousands of households, knocking on doors, introducing himself and asking for support from the voters during his campaign.

The longtime Socialist won in a traditionally right-leaning area, garnering 58 percent of the vote. His life has been a whirlwind of activity ever since.

To wit, he has helped the usher the community through the devastation wrought by the deadly earthquake of 2010.

He's participated in a precedent-setting, but ultimately unsuccessful, lawsuit involving the 2009 Transparency Law that sought to gain access to public officials' emails.

He's started to work with Chinese companies that want to invest in the area that has traditionally relied heavily on agriculture to power its economy.

He's begun working on a hospital to replace the current facility that, along with other public services, attracts people from all over, but is not equipped with state-of-the-art facilities.

Along with elected officials in nearby San Antonio, he's laid the groundwork to create a distinct governmental region that would seek to release the "super-centralized" system that, not unlike Chicago in Illinois, concentrates a disproportionate amount of power and resources in the largest city.

He's supporting Michelle Bachelet so that she can win in the first round in the upcoming presidential elections as well as backing other candidates with similar political leanings.

He's also raising a family.

Dunreith and I spent three and a half hours with him this morning and afternoon.

I had previously met Mario briefly at Diego Portales University with Alberto Barrera, a former MIRista, friend and husband of colleague and guide Alejandra Matus. We were following up on his invitation for us to visit his community.

Dunreith and I took the Route 78 bus from the San Borja bus station for a peaceful, hour-long ride through increasingly green, hilly and rural territory to arrive near the town square.

After walking to the town square and looking for the municipal building, we received help from Juan Manuel Cornejo, a hale and hearty lifetime Melepilla resident who works in real estate. Cornejo delivered us to the mayor's office and took his leave after passing me a business card.

Dressed in a sweater and blue jeans, Mario is close to six feet with thinning, fine black hair. He is clean-shaven, and emits a look of intense concentration on his face as he listens.

Mario speaks quietly and moves and acts in an efficient, economical fashion. He used the time the town's lawyer came in to talk with us about the transparency lawsuit to rapidly sign a bunch of documents, all the while continuing to follow the conversation. His phone buzzes constantly with calls and texts and emails.

The Social Democrat came of age during the 1988 plebiscite in which the Chilean electorate voted to end the reign of dictator Augusto Pinochet. Then 17 years old, he couldn't vote, but he was able to throw himself into the work and see the value of a key opportunity converted into a meaningful social result.

The pictures on the wall in his office show that his political commitments and high levels of energy have remained largely the same since then.

On one wall is a framed copy of the Bolivarian dream of a pan-Latin American federation.

On an adjacent wall is an arpillera, or tapestry, that were common forms of resistance during the Pinochet dictatorship. (He later gave Dunreith nine cards with multi-colored cloth Nativity scenes.) Near that are three black and white pictures he received during a recent trip to Cuba.

Gebauer's emotional scars from that era remain.

Over lunch, Dunreith said that she has been watching *Los 80*, Andrés Wood's company's representation of life during the dictatorship as experienced by a single family.

"I watched one episode of the show and decided not to watch more," Mario said. His choice was not because the program has inaccuracies. Quite the opposite, in fact. He praised the scenes and clothes and music and television excerpts that appear in the episodes.

Rather the show brings back painful memories for Mario. He didn't elaborate, but said, simply, "Era fuerte."

It was strong.

His words came after we had spoken in the office about the major initiatives he has been engaged in during his first term and the beginning of his second four years in office. Mario explained that he is deeply committed to bringing public investment to Melipilla. It's no easy task, as about 80 percent of the municipalities have no such investment. He estimates that he travels to Santiago about once a week to solicit funds, among other purposes.

We had arrived at lunch after driving in the mayor's official car, a white pickup truck, past rolling hills with vineyards, horses, cows, basic houses with Chilean flags and road signs with campaign pictures of candidates like Juan Antonio Coloma.

Don Roberto, a brown-haired lifelong native of Melipilla, drove, and then ate, with us at El Mirador de Popeta, a restaurant that sits above the main highway on a dusty and winding road and that specializes in typical seafood.

Miriam, an energetic grandmother of three with a purple sweater, thick black hair in a ponytail and amiable manner, greeted Gebauer with a familiar hug and ushered us to our table.

We were the only ones in the restaurant.

Shortly after we sat down, Miriam brought a steaming pile of the largest, tastiest seafood appetizer I've ever shared. Shrimp, scallops, mussels in shells that ringed that the black, cast-iron bowl. Large pieces of salmon and reinata. Vegetables and a rich, brown soy-based sauce underneath.

And, of course, a pisco sour. This one had a touch of ginger on the top that added a tangy twist.

We spoke during the meal about what the experience of people in the area was during the dictatorship. Don Roberto explained that many people worked on farms, and received their information about what was happening from their patron, or boss, and thus did not know about the atrocities the Pinochet regime had committed. Because of that, the recent commemorative activities and shows on television had been a potent and disturbing revelation, he said.

In between peppering us throughout the drive and meal about the American political situation, Gebauer told us about visiting the Holocaust Memorial in Israel, his trips to Rio and his sense of Buenos Aires.

Miriam came back after we had finished—she told me she was going to punish me because I hadn't eaten enough—and asked if we wanted dessert. We chatted for a minute about El Mirador, which gets its seafood and shellfish from Santiago and which she and her husband opened two years ago. By this time the restaurant was bustling with customers. The opening came 40 years into their marriage and decades after her husband, who worked for most of his life in restaurant kitchens, first hatched his dream.

Miriam told us that her daughter has taught English for nine years. "But the English of England, not America, which is a lower form," Mario said.

"It's like the difference between Castilian and Chilean Spanish," I answered. (We had already discussed how many Chileans pride themselves on speaking a Spanish that is generously called "hard to understand".)

They laughed loudly.

"The Americans are the Chileans of English," I added.

More laughter.

We talked a little while longer until a pause came in the conversation.

"Shall we go?" Mario asked.

It was a statement more than a question. We got back in the car. Mario talked, texted and answered as we drove. Don Roberto dropped us off at the bus station.

Toward the end of the meal, Mario had said he hoped to get back to his studies next year.

I wouldn't count on it.

Carlo Gutiérrez and the Fight for Public Emails

Posted on October 2, 2013

Carlo Gutiérrez, head of the legal team in Melipilla.
(Photo courtesy of Jeff Kelly Lowenstein)

As part of my work as a Fulbright scholar here in Santiago I'm looking at the impact of the landmark 2009 Transparency Law on investigative reporting.

However, I changed the focus of my research changed after I arrived and found that my initial plan of doing a pre-and post-law analysis of content in the country's leading news outlet was fundamentally flawed. Instead, I'm taking the pulse of a range of folks who have been involved with the law.

Carlo Gutiérrez, who heads the legal team of the municipality of Melipilla, is one of them. We met briefly last week during our meeting with Melipilla Mayor Mario Gebauer.

Gutiérrez was the point person for the municipality's ultimately unsuccessful effort to gain access to emails that contained communication about how to distribute reconstruction funds after the devastating earthquake of February 2010.

I took the bus again to Melipilla, made my way to the city hall, and was directed to the back of a series of single-story buildings. After asking three people for directions, I found Gutiérrez's modest office. His name is printed on the wooden door. Neatly organized piles of paper sit like rows of cards in a solitaire game. Gutiérrez, who has a boyish face and longish black hair, arrived a couple of minutes after I did.

He had prepared a folder of material relative to the precedent-setting case he had filed and that led him eventually to present for the first time in his life before the country's Supreme Court.

For Gutiérrez, who had previously worked in the Interior Department, the initial request as well as the subsequent legal arguments, seemed straightforward.

The Transparency Law gives citizens the right to information by and about their public officials. Digital communication like emails that are written from official accounts are covered by the law.

The subsecretary of the Interior, then, had a responsibility to supply the information Gutiérrez had requested on behalf of the community.

It didn't go that simply.

Gutiérrez explained that the agency answered neither the first nor the second request he sent. When they eventually did answer, they refused to provide the information, citing privacy concerns of the public officials.

This struck Gutiérrez as strange because they explicitly had asked for information from public officials written on public accounts about public business.

The community then appealed to the Transparency Council established by the law. It accepted the municipality's argument and said that it had a right to the emails it had requested.

This time the government appealed to the regional court in Santiago. It's the middle of three levels within the Chilean court system.

Gutiérrez offered an oral argument before the court. Again, he felt the issue at hand from a legal perspective was straightforward. But the court of three judges found otherwise. It held in favor of the defendants, accepting the argument that emails written by public officials on public accounts are not subject to the law.

On to the Supreme Court, the highest in the land.

Gutiérrez again went and presented his oral argument. A lawyer for the Transparency Council joined him. As opposed to the United States, where lawyers arguing before the Supreme Court have exactly 30 minutes and can be peppered by questions from any of the nine justices, in Chile the lawyers have about an hour, Gutiérrez said.

Also in contrast with the United States, where the questions the judges ask often can reveal the justice's orientation in a case, Gutiérrez explained that the lawyers only received a few questions, none of which sparked a meaningful exchange.

Earlier this year the court rendered its decision. It held in favor of the defendants.

The decision was a bitter disappointment to Gutiérrez, who felt that it was made for political reasons. The court has reiterated its stance in ensuing cases filed by non-profit organizations like Ciudadano Inteligente. But what is perhaps of even graver concern is that Secretary General Cristián Larroulet is seeking to codify in law the restrictions that the court has placed through the cases on which it has ruled.

In Chile, legislation originates from the executive branch, then goes to the Congress and Senate for discussion and a vote before returning to the president to be signed. As Secretary General, Larroulet has President Sebastián Piñera's ear and is doing his bidding. (Piñera already showed his anti-access position in 2011 when he sought to have members of the Transparency Council removed because of their support for releasing emails.)

Gutiérrez holds some hope on the new government that he hopes will propose legislation that goes in a more, rather than less, open direction. But he also is strongly concerned that the courts' actions have struck a strong blow against the nation's still fragile democracy.

"Chile has been an authoritarian country in the past," Gutiérrez said. "A key tool in the transition to democracy is the access to information."

"They have closed the window on that," he said, a trace of sadness crossing his face.

Rafael Gumucio's Book Launch

Posted on September 29, 2013

Rafael Gumucio's latest book.
(Photo courtesy of Jeff Kelly Lowenstein)

Now that's what I call a book launch.

The event was held in the basement of the Gabriela Mistral Center, or GAM. Named for one of Chile's two Nobel Prize-winning poets, the center was opened during the tenure of Salvador Allende, and was the place where the ruling junta went after the Pinochet coup. Renamed the Diego Portales Building during the dictatorship, the center resumed its art-oriented focus after Pinochet's reign ended.

As opposed to similar events in the United States, where the author is introduced, speaks, reads a few sections of the book and answers some questions, author, Diego Portales University neighbor and friend Rafael Gumucio didn't speak until an hour into the event, and ultimately did not read a single word from *A Personal History of Chile*, his latest work.

This was because he only spoke after Carlos Peña, the rector of our university and one of Chile's top newspaper columnists, had read his opening remarks in which he discussed Rafael's weaving of fantastic pairings of important figures in Chilean history as similar to legendary Argentine author Jorge Luis Borges' *Ficciones*.

Rafael began to speak directly after eminent historian Gabriel Salazar, a white-haired bearded man with a deep voice who speaks in paragraphs, not sentences, had discussed at length a 1998 United Nations human development report that spoke about the contrast between Chile's economic success and "malestar interior," or internal discomfort.

Salazar talked about the directions and reversals within the book, of his use of the Hegelian method of thesis-antithesis-synthesis, and of how, for Rafael, former President Ricardo Lagos was similar to Napoleon for Hegel.

When he finally spoke, Rafael, who has wild black hair, a full beard that is flecked with grey near his chin and was wearing a blue jacket with a dark sweater, unleashed a torrent of words, ideas and jokes.

I don't know Rafael really well and I have not yet read the book. Our offices in the journalism department at Diego Portales University stand around the corner from each other. I sat in on a panel he moderated about the role and limits of humor in Chilean society—he's the head of the Institute of Humor Studies at the University—and we both attended a lunch for author and futurist Nicco Mele that Alejandra Matus organized. I did know that he had been exiled to France during the dictatorship. But even these comparatively meager interactions were enough to help me understand that he combines the frenetic energy and wit of Robin Williams with the humor of Roberto Benigni.

As Rafael riffed about his pairing of epic Chilean figures like Pinochet and television host Don Francisco, about how he had thought ex-president Ricardo Lagos would govern compared with what he actually did and about how Michelle Bachelet would like to be anti-colonial, but is in fact colonial,

I turned around and looked at the room, which was filled with close to 100 people in seats and standing against the back wall. They were listening and, in many cases, they were smiling a pleased, even indulgent, smile.

So, too, was Rafael's father, whose name Rafael bears. The elder Gumucio was sitting, along with his wife, daughter-in-law and other family members, in a section of chairs to his son's right.

As he spoke, Rafael's younger daughter, a binky in her mouth and pigtails on her head, moved back and forth from her grandfather to her father's lap. She stayed just long enough to crawl up, get a hug and then return to her grandfather. Back and forth she went, sometimes crawling when her father was speaking, at other times when he was listening to the other panelists.

Rafael Gumucio with his younger daughter at the GAM.
(Photo courtesy of Jeff Kelly Lowenstein)

The conversation dipped and turned, ebbed and flowed back and forth among the panelists and the author and moderator, moving deep into the nature of history and social movements and the country's real and imagined past. Broadcast journalist Consuelo Saavedra was just asking

Rafael one of many questions she still had when the word came that the time for the program had ended.

No one left.

We all repaired to the area outside the room, where Rafael signed books and talked with people as the rest of us dolloped corn kernels onto sopaipillas, picked up and munched eggplants on crunchy bread, and, of course, drank some red wine.

After a while, I hugged and congratulated Rafael before walking out into the cool night to head onto the Metro and back to Dunreith. As I walked, I realized anew that Chile is a still-wounded country engaged in healing from the damage caused by the the physical pain and enforced silence of the dictatorship.

Humor is an important part of that process.

I thought about the gift that Rafael has given of embracing and moving into the intersection of personal history with public experience, and of launching the book in the very building where those most responsible for that damage first announced their seizure of power.

And, once more, I appreciated my great fortune to be in Chile at this moment in its history, and to be a witness to an event where university presidents and scholars and humorists and friends and family can sit and talk and listen and laugh in a way that would have been unimaginable just a generation ago.

Striking Workers and Santiago's Central Markets

Posted on August 16, 2013

A striking Chilean postal worker fishing for a dignified salary.
(Photo courtesy of Jeff Kelly Lowenstein)

When Dunreith and I read about Santiago's fabled trio of markets of Mercado Central, Tirso de Molina, and La Vega Central, one consistent message stood out: watch your wallets closely as pickpockets are everywhere and they'll take your money.

It turns out that the warning was far too limited as other dangers are lurking. We discovered this today after walking from our apartment to the market.

Along the way we passed a lively postal workers' strike in which red-shirted and red-jacketed employees were blowing high-pitched whistles, chanting and hanging signs near Pio Nono, a major Santiago bridge.

Some of the more adventurous strikers had used a rope to propel themselves down to the edge of the Mapocho River, where they danced, sang and held up more signs.

One worker had a sign on the end of a fishing pole that explained he was fishing for a decent salary.

Unlike in the United States, where the current Chicago Public Schools' teacher strike makes national news, organized labor here is more willing to strike frequently on local and national levels. In addition to the postal workers, garbage workers, miners, workers at the world's largest ground-based telescope and the entire city of Tocopilla, a city in the northern region of Antofagasta, all have gone on strike just since we landed here in mid-July.

We passed by a trio of workers in a nearby park huddling around a tree and counting donations they had received and, a little while later, we arrived at Mercado Central. Once there and in the other two markets, we learned that you actually have to watch out for all manner of hazards while you're in all three places.

Dangers like a massive side of beef being toted on a worker's back as he hustles toward a nearby butchery.

Like cardboard packages flying from one end of a truck to another as you walk past it.

Like being sandwiched by dozen of boxes being pulled along by a pair of workers, one of whom is talking on a cell phone, going in opposite directions.

Like the startling image of a pig's head with skin and an even more arresting cow's skull without, eyes protruding and the tongue hanging out to one side.

Like a bicycle that can run over your Achilles' heel and a car that can run over your foot, if not your entire body.

Like waiters in restaurants bustling by with arms full of clean or empty plates.

This of course says nothing about the sea of people who walk, jostle and bump you as you make your way through and around the stalls, rows and exterior of the three buildings that take up a few city blocks.

A cow's head in La Vega.
(Photo courtesy of Jeff Kelly Lowenstein)

Yet navigating these obstacles is not only an integral part of the market experience, doing so allows you to enter a fantastic zone with a ferocious variety of smells and a seemingly limitless range of fish, meat, fowl, produce, potatoes, and household items carefully arrayed in a delicious splash of precision and color.

Each market has its specialty.

Mercado Central is the fish market.

Tirso de Molina has absolutely scrumptious natural juices made right in front of you and to which you can add sugar, vitamins, milk, or nothing at all.

La Vega has a certain swagger—a mural stated emphatically that after gods there is La Vega—and has an endless supply of fruit stands to complete the beef, pork and poultry sections.

I got a raspberry fruit juice with milk at Tirso, and will definitely be back to head up to the second floor to sample a cazuela, a typical Chilean dish with beef or chicken, a potato, rice and vegetables in a piping hot broth, for 1500 pesos, or three dollars.

Meanwhile, Dunreith got a kilogram of clementines for 300 pesos, a total of 60 cents.

Reading the charges for food and meals at the markets was a bit like Plato's Allegory of the Cave, in which my realizing that the prices I had been extolling in our Providencia Market were not quite as inexpensive as I had thought was parallel to thinking that the shadows in the cave were actually light.

For instance, a mushroom and cheese empanada that costs 1200 peso, or $2.40, in Mercado Providencia around the corner from our house, goes for just 780, or about $1.60 at the central markets.

The lower prices are just one part of the place's appeal.

I asked the short, black-haired woman with piercing eyes who owned the stand where the meal that she stopped eating to serve us had come from.

"They come from the fields in buses that stop outside the building," she told me.

"Your meal?" I repeated.

"Oh, no, that's from upstairs," she chuckled." I thought you were asking about the fruit."

"So the fruit comes from the trucks, the meal comes from upstairs and you come from Santiago?" I asked.

"Of course," she replied." I'm Santiaguina."

"Pura Santiaguina," I said.

One hundred percent.

"One hundred percent," she affirmed.

Another fruit stand we walked by was playing a scene from *Destilando Amor*, the Mexican telenovela that starred future Mexican First Lady Angélica Rivera and Eduardo Yañez as Gaviota and Rodrigo, a tequila worker and scion who fall in love with each other.

In 2007 I learned how to speak Spanish by watching the novela with Dunreith. I told the owner of this stand, another woman, the story, then pointed to Dunreith and said, "This is my Gaviota."

"This is my Rodrigo," Dunreith replied, pointing her thumb at me.

We all laughed.

After a couple of hours, Dunreith and I began the walk back to our apartment.

We were crossing the street in the Baquedano neighborhood when a striking postal worker stepped in front of us and implored us to support their cause. Dunreith obliged, reaching into her pocket and dropping a coin that clinked as it landed in the tin can.

We had managed to not get pickpocketed at the markets, but hadn't avoided paying a price, albeit willingly, along the way home.

Pamela Betancur's Unvanquished Dream

Posted on December 7, 2013

Pamela Betancur and her son, Juan José Larraguibel,
in the kitchen of their house in a campamento, or shantytown,
in the La Florida neighborhood in Santiago.
(Photo courtesy of Jon Lowenstein/NOOR/Pulitzer Center on Crisis Reporting)

Pamela Betancur's face still fills with light when she starts to recount the dream that drove her in 1999 to borrow money from her friends and cousin to leave her home town of Los Ángeles in Southern Chile for the big city of Santiago.

"I wanted to study and to gain a profession," says Betancur, who stopped attending school around eighth grade.

Her father had never been an active presence in her life. Her mother had died of uterine cancer when Pamela was just 10—a wound that is still fresh more than two decades later. "You have many other relationships in your life, but only with your mother are you a daughter," says Betancur, who has dark black hair that flows below her shoulders.

She could barely contain her excitement when she left Los Ángeles. All she had was the money for the trip and the sack for her clothes her cousin had bought for her. She had packed the fewest clothes necessary and hidden them under her bed. At 6:00 a.m she had snuck out of the house where she was staying and caught the only bus available for that day.

Her enthusiasm continued when she arrived in Santiago and stayed at a friend's house. But after a week the friend told her she had to leave and her troubles began.

She found work as a housekeeper for an Arab family who made her work from 5:30 a.m. to 11:00 p.m. and yelled at her for her inability to cook the food they wanted.

"I didn't know," she says, wincing slightly at the memory.

One day, about two months into her time there, Pamela started crying uncontrollably.

"I couldn't do it anymore," she says, simply.

After staying wherever she could—a period that included sleeping at a social service agency—Pamela found a campamento, or shantytown, in Santiago's La Florida community. The once-established neighborhood had been devastated by a flood in the late 1990s. Little remained but rock and rubble.

Pamela started to build a house. She's been in La Florida since.

She got a major boost about 10 years ago. That's when her brother Rubis, whom her mother named after a famous singer, moved to Santiago and joined her.

Together they've expanded the house, which is built from sheets of wood from wherever they can find them and powered by electricity diverted from the local power grid. The extended family drinks water from a poached source. They've saved and scrimped and installed a television, bought a computer for her eight-year-old son Juan José, and purchased a washing machine.

We met Pamela while we were visiting the campamento to observe the work of TECHO, a Chilean-based non-profit that works with vulnerable communities to diagnose, and then help them meet, their needs.

After a while she invited us behind the wall that encased the two-story house. We walked into the yard. A cousin was washing and rinsing a rug by hand. An empty barbeque grill stood against one of the walls.

The ceilings were quite short—I am 5'8" and easily touched the ceiling with my hand—and the kitchen was cozy and clean. A wooden staircase led up to the second floor.

Juan José sat on a living room couch, playing a game on the computer as the television droned in the background. A picture of Pamela's mother, his late grandmother, a luminous smile on her face, hung above him.

We talked for a while in the house, which had a quiet hum of activity.

Rubis, who has thick hands, a firm handshake and a scruffy beard, explained how he had learned to install electricity by himself. The mother of his son came in, holding their round-cheeked, serious-looking boy who will soon celebrate his first birthday. One cousin dropped by, then another. Then a niece who lives next door.

Pamela told us that she had just returned from visiting her hometown. Life there is tranquil, the pace of life slower. But as before, she could find no opportunities in one of the country's poorest regions.

Pamela always tells her relatives that everything is going well for her in Santiago so that they don't worry. She brought back a home-grown vegetable specialty that tastes like a mushroom.

Along with other children, Juan José is getting tutored through TECHO. Pamela attends weekly meetings as a member of the local board that represents the campamento with the city's government. She's excited about the construction of the elevated blue and white community center in her neighborhood with an elevated roof built by volunteers wearing blue and red t-shirts.

Work has been erratic for Pamela. The schools aren't great and have far fewer resources than those in other Santiago neighborhoods.

But she still holds firm to the vision that propelled her from her home and into the world.

"I believe I can do it," she says.

The Pulitzer Center on Crisis Reporting supported this story.

Returning Home to Chicago

Posted on December 27, 2013

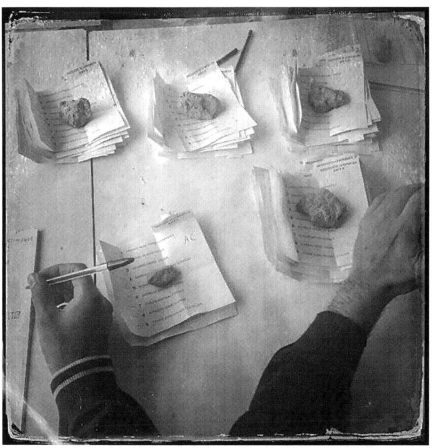

Some of the 6.6 million votes counted on Sunday, November 17.
(Photo courtesy of Jon Lowenstein/NOOR/Pulitzer Center on Crisis Reporting)

We're in the air from Toronto to Chicago.

We've left Santiago, site of fulfilled dreams, 80-degree Christmas Days, our impossibly dusty postage stamp of an apartment, and the consumption of more pisco sours and glasses, well, bottles, of red wine than we could have ever imagined, and are heading back to the Windy City that has been our home since 2002.

With grins that stretched beyond our ears, Dunreith and I deposited the check from the house sale we completed the day before we left on our Chilean adventure.

It far exceeded our greatest expectations.

We had the great privilege of being in Chile as the nation confronted, more directly than ever before, the still-raw wounds from the Pinochet coup that happened on September 11, 1973.

We attended vigils and memorials and events and plays and conferences and documentary films and panels and book launches, all of which were dedicated to grappling with the enduring impact of the overthrow of democratically-elected Salvador Allende and the brutal aftermath.

I've lived in the United States close to 50 years, but never before had I witnessed the concentrated and unified focusing on a single event in our nation's history the way Chileans from Arica in the north to Punta Arenas at the end of the world turned their attention to the coup.

In October we witnessed the jubilant eruption of emotion issuing forth from Chileans who hugged, kissed, screamed and honked their horns when their beloved soccer team punched its ticket to the world's largest sport event, to be held next June in Brazil.

In November we went to election events and talked to voters of all persuasions and ages and sides of the political spectrum during what turned out to be the first of two rounds in the presidential elections.

And in December we traveled to Torres del Paine, a national park of unsurpassed and staggering beauty that recently was named the eighth wonder of the world, when Michelle Bachelet made history in becoming the first candidate ever to be elected president twice in the post-democracy era.

Beyond these momentous months in Chilean history, we received an enormously generous reception from Chileans with whom we had some connection—we met everyone from dear friend Marjorie Agosín's seemingly inexhaustible supply of cousins and former students to a female anesthetist Dad had helped train nearly 30 years ago to our colleague, friend of a friend, guide/secret weapon Alejandra Matus—and those whom we had the good fortune to meet through our travels.

My Data Journalism students at Diego Portales University gradually understood my Spanish, my teaching methods and the concepts and application of this type of journalism in a process that left both sides feeling enriched for the encounter.

My research into the landmark 2009 Transparency Act, after an initial shift in focus, led me to talk with journalists, lawyers, non-profit executives, government representatives and plain folks in a project that gave me a sharper sense of the law's as yet incompletely realized potential.

Dunreith and I traveled to the vineyards of the Central Valley, and to the coast cities of Valparaíso and Viña del Mar. With our son Aidan we flew to the searing desert of San Pedro de Atacama, the world's driest such space, and to Patagonia, a place Dunreith had longed to visit for years.

We also ventured to Rio, where I had the honor of attending, teaching and presenting to colleagues at the Global Investigative Journalism Conference who are doing investigative work, often at great physical peril, throughout the world.

We flew to Buenos Aires, where we met Dad and Lee before they set off on a two-week tour to Southern Argentina and up through Chile, and strolled together down elegant, inordinately wide, European-style boulevards, ate ice cream at Café Tortoni, the continent's oldest cafe that oozes with swagger, listened and learned for three hours at ESMA, the largest of the Argentine dictator's network of detention centers, and feasted on the sights and food of El Ateneo, the former theater that has been converted into one of the world's most spectacular bookstores.

My brother Jon and I had the tremendous fortune to receive a grant from the Pulitzer Center to do a project about the impact of the past on the present in Chile 40 years after the coup. Together we worked long hours over the course of two weeks for a three-part series that ran on *The New Yorker's* Photo Booth and on *Hoy's* website.

The family visits over our final six weeks in the country helped confirm to me the possibility of weaving together the people and passions and dreams and values that I hold most dear. Perhaps, greatest of all, it's fortified my increasing conviction that this way of living is not only possible, but could in a very real sense become ordinary.

My brother and ace photographer Jon Lowenstein in action.
(Photo courtesy of Jon Lowenstein/NOOR/Pulitzer Center on Crisis Reporting)

Now, we are returning to Chicago, the city from which we left, where we raised Aidan from a boy to a man, and where we have spent the vast majority of our married life.

I am, and will always be, a Bostonian at my core. I had too many seminal events, from the Blizzard of '78 to the 1975 World Series to growing up amidst that inimitable accent for it to ever be otherwise. But if Boston in my heart, Chicago's in my guts.

The people's straightforward manner and generous spirit, the city's sense of itself as a place of story and legend, the passion that Chicagoans bring to their sports and their politics and their brats and their neighborhoods, its industrial past and tortured history with race and segregation and immigration and labor that make it what the late, great Studs Terkel called "the true American city", have all gotten in deep, and are not going anywhere, either.

I'll miss our life in Santiago and our travels throughout the country and continent, to be sure.

And I'm excited to fly over the leafless trees toward the dirtied snow and land at O'Hare, to walk in the 20-degree weather and see our breath and our circle of friends and family again, and to bring a fresh, broader perspective to my ongoing love for the city.

We don't know our exact next steps, or, frankly, where we're going to live after we stay at Jon's place on the South Side.

But we do know without any shred of a doubt that, as always, the adventure will continue.

Acknowledgments

This book is testament to the truth that no one does anything significant on his own.

In June of 2012 I was talking about my desire to go to Chile with Joe Germuska, who was then with the Chicago Tribune's NewsApps team.

Joe directed me to Miguel Paz, an extraordinary journalism innovator and a Chilean who had taught at Diego Portales University. Miguel connected me to Department Chair Carlos Aldunate, who then wrote the necessary letter of invitation.

Beth Macy, a friend and a remarkable writer, introduced me to Alejandra Matus, her Nieman classmate and "sweet sister." Alejandra, her husband Alberto Barrera and her son Alejandro could not have been more generous to Dunreith and me throughout our time in their country. Alejandra's advice was so effective I called her my "arma secreta," or secret weapon! The whole university community showed us a warm welcome during our stay. Loreto Correa gave me wise counsel and warm support, as did Josefa Romero. My colleagues in the Journalism department invariably treated me as one of the group, not as an outsider. This remarkable group included Patricia de la Rivera, Carolina Gainza, Andrea Insunza, Javier Ortega, Arly Faundes, Jorge González, Nicole Etchegaray, Andrés Scherman and Rafael Gumucio.

In addition to writing this generous introduction, Hugo Rojas was an unfailing source of insight about Chile's ongoing grappling with memory, books, people to consult and restaurant recommendations. He and his wife Kiki could not have been more kind to us. Stacey Platt introduced me to Hugo in 2008 and has been a source of inspiration and friendship since we first we first met more than a decade ago.

The folks at the Fulbright Commission were a fountain of information, insight and good cheer. Yunuen Varela was a booster of the blog that forms the basis of this book from nearly the first post and told us about the Fulbright Specialist program in which I later participated. Antonio Campaña graciously created time and space for me to share the findings of my transparency research and told us about the critical importance of the words "Reserva" and "Gran Reserva." Victoria Viteri reached out out to us about all kinds of events in Santiago and beyond and has maintained contact since we returned to the United States in December 2013.

My Fulbright classmates swapped notes about banks, trips and students, attended yoga classes, drank piscos and Terremotos and supported each other through our adventures. I am grateful to all of them, particularly Larry Geri.

As she did with my previous book, Virginia Freed turned her attentive and loving eye to many of the entries. Karen Rutter did outstanding work on this front, too, and Barbara Ludman chipped in on several pieces. Chris Moore did a superlative job with design in the second project of what I'm confident will be an ongoing relationship. Robert Smart and the team at the Center for Scholarly and Creative Excellence at Grand Valley State University, where I teach, supported the copy editing, production and distribution processes.

For close to 20 years Marjorie Agosín has been a friend, mentor and inspiration. Her passion and love for her home country was part of what inspired our many-year quest to get there. She tried to help us find housing, connected us to her cousins Roberto Agosín and Sylvia Broder and generally exulted at the wonder of the home she had left so many years ago. Friends and *Hoy* bosses Fernando Diaz and John Trainor gave me a gift for which I will always be grateful when they backed my application to the Fulbright program.

Friend and fellow believer in the power of information and connecting good people Mark Hallett and his lovely wife Carmen Vidal-Hallett introduced us to Miguel Huerta and Macarena Rodriguez over pizza at their home. Between the two of them they picked us up at the airport, lent us bicycles, showed us around the city and spoke at my first and final class of the semester.

I loved working with all of the students in my Data Journalism class who engaged with new material, called me "profe" and tolerated my Spanish and their discomfort as we covered new material that challenged their previous way of doing journalism.

As with all major life ventures, my family has given me unconditional love and unstinting support. Dunreith and I met my father Edward Lowenstein and his life partner Lee Kass for several enormously enjoyable days in Buenos Aires as they opened their tour of South America before ending it in Santiago about two weeks later.

My brother Jon Lowenstein came to Santiago after we had secured support from the Pulitzer Center on Crisis Reporting for us to work on a three-part series for *The New Yorker*, among other publications. Waking up each day for two weeks and saying, "I've got to go to work, honey. I'm on assignment with Jon for the *The New Yorker*," was a life thrill I will not soon, if ever, forget.

Our son Aidan joined us after his semester in New Zealand ended and we spent a month together during which we ventured to the southernmost point of the continent and spent time in the spectacular Torres del Paine.

Dunreith Kelly Lowenstein spearheaded the sale of our house that took place the day before we boarded the flight to Santiago, and as always has provided inspiration, challenge and infinite love. She supported me from before I filed my first application to be a Fulbright Scholar in 2000 to spend a semester in Tanzania, and has continued every day since then. She has my deepest love and gratitude.

Above all, I am grateful to all of the Chilean people I met who let me into their homes and hearts. It is to them that this book is dedicated.

About the Author

Jeff Kelly Lowenstein is an assistant professor at Grand Valley State University in Allendale, Michigan. His work has been published in The New Yorker and the Center for Public Integrity, among many publications, and has earned national and international recognition. In 2013 he and his wife Dunreith lived in Santiago, Chile, where Jeff was a Fulbright Scholar for a semester at Diego Portales University. *The Chilean Chronicles* is his fourth book.

NOTES